SWEET MADNESS

Sweet Madness

A Study of Humor

By WILLIAM F. FRY, Jr.

PACIFIC BOOKS, Publishers
Palo Alto, California

First *Pacific Books Paperbounds* edition published 1968.

Library of Congress catalog card No. 63-17821.

International Standard Book Number 0-87015-163-0.

Manufactured in the United States of America.

PACIFIC BOOKS, *Publishers*
P.O. Box 558
Palo Alto, California 94302

This book

is lovingly dedicated

to my Wife

Preface

This book is a distillation of thoughts and findings encountered in the process of working as Research Assistant in the Department of Anthropology at Stanford University. I was working in association with Gregory Bateson and the other members of our research staff in an exploration of the functions of the paradoxes of abstraction in implicit communication, humor, mental illness, psychotherapy, and culture. Our project was financed by a grant from the Rockefeller Foundation during 1952-1954 and one from the Josiah Macy, Jr. Foundation during 1955-1958.

The first part of the book, consisting of two chapters, serves mainly as a very general introduction to the subject of humor. The second part is a group of four chapters which have little apparent interrelationship (except that they are all about humor, in one way or another). Weakly related as they are, however, these chapters serve to introduce a variety of ideas important to the climax, and concluding part, of the book. This third part is divided into two closely connected chapters—one historical and the other expositive. These chapters are the real raison d'être of the book and present the theory of the structure of humor that developed during my research studies mentioned above.

I was guided and assisted by many persons during this investigation--principally by Gregory Bateson, but also by Jay Haley and John Weakland, research colleagues; Dr. Don D. Jackson of the Palo Alto Clinic,

viii SWEET MADNESS

Palo Alto, California; Dr. Richard Walters of the University of California, at Los Angeles; the late Dr. Victor Gonda; Dr. Luis Lombardo of Mexico City and Dr. Robert B. Aird of the University of California, San Francisco; Carey Baldwin, director of the Fleishhacker Zoo, San Francisco; and by my wife, Elizabeth S. Fry. The Bibliography of works from which I have drawn data, suggestions, and associations is at the back of this volume; I wish to mention especially, in this context, Expression of the Emotions in Man and Animals, by Charles Darwin, and Communication, by Gregory Bateson and Jurgen Ruesch.

It is my pleasure to express my deep appreciation to Mr. Bateson for his invaluable help in editing the manuscript and to Miss Genevieve Lefevre and Mrs. Edith Bridges for their fine work at the typewriter.

William F. Fry, Jr.

March 8, 1963

Table of Contents

Preface   vii

PART ONE

   I. A Survey of Humor   3
  II. Problems in Humor   26

PART TWO

 III. A Metaphoric Discussion.   41
  IV. The Unconscious   57
   V. Levels of Living   69
  VI. The Uses of Humor   90

PART THREE

 VII. Background for Theory.   119
VIII. Humor's Anatomy.   137

Bibliography   173

PART ONE

CHAPTER I

A Survey of Humor

A Zen Buddhist monk asked Rynkon Zenji, "How is it that Pindola, who has only one body, moves about the four quarters of the universe accepting alms?" The Zenji replied, "The moons upon a thousand rivers are the print of only one moon; ten thousand houses over all the land greet the spring at the same time."

A newly married man requested professional help for a problem of impotence. A fundamental part of his therapy consisted of his being congratulated on the intensity of his admiration for his bride—so intense as to suspend all ordinary response to her presence.

Each of us, from time to time, finds it useful to regard familiar phenomena in a new way. In this volume on humor the reader finds some novel approaches to a subject quite old and very familiar.

Unfortunately, there is no simple agreement as to the time of origin of humor in a person's life. There is considerable controversy over whether humor[1] develops

---

[1] The word "humor" is being used in a generic sense. I am arbitrarily utilizing this word—as other words such as "comedy," "the ludicrous," "wit," have been used by other authors—throughout this book to indicate all phenomena associated, in an essential manner, with that elusive emotion variously named amusement, amused pleasure, humor, fun, merriment, joviality, etc. While it is true that, in some contexts, it is important to differentiate between, say, fun and wit, or

during infancy or whether it is an adult prerogative. A considerable number of people hold the opinion that humor is not humor except as defined in the adult sense. Others are firmly convinced that children, as well as adults, enjoy humor. It can easily be agreed, however, that those phenomena most closely linked with humor— i.e., smiling and laughter—appear quite early in life. Smiling and laughter appear in the infant's repertoire in certain situations within weeks of the beginning of life. They continue through childhood until they eventually accompany adult humor. From that period on, the association is perpetuated—with certain exceptions— until death.

One hesitates to estimate the frequency of the occurrence of humor. I achieved some recognition of the complexity of this task during the process of the research that contributed many of the ideas presented in this book. As a part of research activity, a I set myself the assignment of discovering the number of smiles and laughs that came to me during the course of an eight-hour period.

The experiment lasted only six of the proposed eight hours. By the end of the sixth hour, it had become obvious to me that certain factors which defied compromise were operating to make valueless any statistical results derived from the procedure. These factors introduced serious distortions into the experimental situation.

I found that I became too self-conscious. I would become aware of an impending smile and prepare to record it. But, in my anticipating it, it would fail to appear. I had entered a different mood. The intention of recording the smile contributed to the moment in

---

(Footnote continued)
amusement and comedy, etc., I shall by and large either avoid these contexts or, for the particular instance, specify the various subgenera under consideration. In most instances where "humor" appears, the definition refers to humor in the adult world. Rarely, "humor" will refer to manifestations—e.g., smiling and laughter—rather than to the general category.

such a manner as to alter its nature and puncture the humor.

During the six hours of the experiment, I made several attempts to manipulate this self-awareness so that it would no longer present such an operational difficulty. These attempts were, by and large, unsuccessful. Only by introducing a "playful mood" was I able to diminish the stifling effect of the scientific context. I proposed to record each smile and laugh "playfully," rather than seriously, and found that fewer of the smiles were inhibited. This manipulation was only partly successful. There were many smiles that died unborn.

This experiment re-emphasized to me the intimate nature of humor as it appears in our lives. Humor becomes such an integral part of the ongoing life process[2] that recording its occurrence forces one to an unnatural degree of self-consciousness. The self-consciousness then operates to create a different mood, and humor has gone.

It is impossible to be simply spontaneous and simply thoughtful at the same time. These two states are mutually exclusive. When one is objective, to any extent, about himself and his spontaneous behavior, a state far more complex than the state of simple spontaneity—or simple thoughtfulness, for that matter—is present. Spontaneous behavior is one level of existence. When a person is aware of that behavior, thinks about himself, another level of existence is introduced. He can become aware of his being aware of himself. And so on, to an infinity of abstraction.

Most of us achieve, with practice and maturation, a delicate balancing of spontaneity and self-watchfulness, with the ongoing life process flowing on relatively smoothly. At certain times, however, as in my

---

[2]The concept of "ongoing life process" is so obvious as to present a tendency towards obscurity. For background reading on the subject, the reader is referred to the chapter on "Selective Inattention" in Harry Stack Sullivan's Clinical Studies in Psychiatry.

experiment, this skill is presented with a serious challenge. My experimentation weighted the awareness side and the balance was lost in an excess of self-consciousness.

Humor is familiar to most people both through its early appearance and persistence, and through its intimate occurrence in their lives. It has been a popular subject for speculation throughout recorded history. As one can confirm by reference to various bibliographies of the humor literature—in, for example, The Psychology of Laughter and Comedy, by V. Y. T. Greig, or Argument of Laughter, by D. H. Munro—there are numerous volumes dealing with various sides of the humor problem.

It is a peculiar characteristic of humor that, despite its popularity as a subject for philosophy, there are many fundamental questions about it that remain unanswered. These questions are the subject of the next chapter.

As did the Zen master who spoke of "the print of only one moon" and the "ten thousand houses" greeting the spring, the reader of this book will consider humor in several ways that will perhaps seem rather surprising. We start with phenomena that are quite familiar—present since the early weeks of life and so much a part of that life that it is a strain to be objective about them. We shall then apply several novel concepts, with the expectation that the experience will prove to be gratifying.

The relationship between humor and play is a topic that recommends itself for early consideration as one of the foundations on which to build the structure of our speculation. The relationship between humor and play has specific importance in this book. (Later, I shall develop the argument that humor and play differ from certain other natural experiences in that the contexts of humor and play propose what is called a logical paradox.)

There are various ways in which this speculation could be initiated. Life could be viewed as a collection of items—e.g., an aggregate of minutes. Each item can be thought of as separate and with its own individual characteristics. In this way, life could be considered in terms only of its component parts. Humor on one hand and play on the other would each constitute one of those parts. Or life could be seen as a unitary phenomenon which has no separate items, but rather is an all-encompassing oneness. The significance of the whole would then be so great that to think in terms of items or parts would be an offense against natural history. The presence of these alternatives in conceptualizing presents certain similarities to the experience of looking at a mosaic. Should one attend to the individual bits of the mosaic, or should one focus interest on the over-all picture? How broad or how narrow should one's perception and attention be?

A third possibility involves a concentration upon the relationships that exist between the various component parts of life. Using the analogy of the mosaic, we can attend to the individual bits from the standpoint of their interrelationships rather than from the standpoint of their own characteristics, such as color or shape: "Each red tile is surrounded by four gold tiles, resulting in rows of alternating red and gold tiles." This attitude affords one the opportunity of being aware of characteristics of the individual bits without focusing so intently as to be blind to a broader picture. The concept of relationships evokes a readiness to accept the possibility of something more than that which is "in the eye." One could focus on a tile and forget the mosaic, or vice versa. Focusing on relationships, however, creates the psychologic atmosphere that reminds one that there must be both parts and wholes in the description of things. It is this method of focusing on relationships that will first be utilized in discussing humor and play.

That there is relationship between humor and play would be contested by few. Visualized graphically, certain phases of relationship constitute areas in which humor and play can be seen to overlap one another. Consider the mosaic analogy again and expand the representation of play and humor from that of individual mosaic tiles to that of larger patterns in the over-all picture. The mosaic picture is life; the pattern of rows of alternating red and gold tiles now represents humor. The concept is further complicated by placing contiguous to this red-and-gold pattern a pattern of rows of alternating blue and gold tiles. The blue-and-gold pattern will represent play. But these two patterns overlap. They are placed so that the red tiles in the last row of red and gold tiles borrow the gold tiles in the first row of blue and gold tiles in order to satisfy the condition "each red tile is surrounded by four gold tiles." The same is true of the blue-and gold pattern, in that the blue tiles of the first row borrow the gold tiles of the last red-and-gold row to produce the result of each blue tile surrounded by four gold ones. As with these mosaic patterns, play and humor may be described as overlapping in several significant areas, sharing phenomena in a way that it becomes a matter of context as to whether the particular gold tile is apportioned to the red-and-gold or to the blue-and-gold.

The research studies from which this book has sprung have demonstrated the existence of a psychological principle that is an overlap for both humor and play. In Part Three this principle is considered extensively. Briefly, the principle involves the precipitation of a logical paradox indicating humor, and play, as different from certain other phenomena of life—e.g., grief, business, conflict. This type of paradox indicates a particular context for humor and play—as a picture frame indicates a particular context for the art contained within and emphasizes discontinuity of the painting with the wall against which it hangs. Certain other phenomena, such as ritual and hypnotic trance, have similarly been discovered to be characterized by this paradox frame.

A second overlap is smiling and laughter—physiologic accompaniments of both humor and play, and little
else (if we disallow such hybrids as the "nervous gig-
gle," or "laconic smile," or "bitter laughter"). The
presence of the controversy over childhood humor is
one evidence of this overlap. If children did not smile
and laugh during their play (or humor?), one could suggest that children do not participate in humor. Yet,
they certainly do smile and laugh. It becomes quite
difficult at times to determine whether their laughs
punctuate play or indicate the presence of a childish
humor. Without a formal understanding of the distin-
guishing features of humor on one hand and play on the
other, one might be tempted to consider that this overlap is without limits and that it involves the entirety of
both humor and play—that the two are the same.

     Another important overlap of humor and play is
found in the "spontaneous-thoughtful" balance that became such a problem during my experiment of counting
smiles and laughs. That a balance of spontaneity and
thoughtfulness is important, is self-evident. The sad
spectacle of schizophrenia (H.S. Sullivan wrote, "schizophrenia represents a failure to control awareness of
ordinarily unwitting levels of thought"), in which confusion between the ongoing life process and dreaming, and
confusion between the object and the metaphor, intrude
themselves, adds testimony to the importance of this
balance. Both humor and play are particularly sensitive to any shift in spontaneous-thoughtful equilibrium.
Who cannot remember the experience of having the
thought of "What am I laughing at?" rudely puncture a
laugh as it developed? Or the experience of thinking
"I'm too old for this sort of thing" interfere with a few
moments of play with a friendly child. A tendency
toward predominance of self-awareness may precipitate
a runaway. The thoughtfulness may be unintegrated and
spontaneity will be temporarily overwhelmed. Or, vice
versa. Other matters, such as business or oratory,
are more hardy, more resistive to such shifts of pro-
portion. These more resistive items of behavior usually

present little challenge to one's balancing skill. This
is not true of play and humor. They are delicate and
demand much of the individual's skill. Play and humor
are two activities in which the human organism receives practice in maintaining the equilibrium of spontaneity-thoughtfulness.

The area of interpersonal behavior is a fourth area
of overlap for humor and play. Interpersonal relationships are involved in both. It must be admitted that
there is little in life that is not interpersonal. We discover, however, that interpersonal behavior is a particularly potent ingredient of these two phenomena. The
soundness of this discovery is particularly obvious in
the case of play. For humor, the role taken by interpersonal behavior is more obscure. One might tell a
joke, for example, apparently without pertinence to the
ongoing interpersonal process, apparently out of context. We shall discover, however, that this apparent
lack of pertinence is deceptive.

An objection to what is stated above could be found
in the instances of playing by oneself and joking with
oneself. People do laugh or smile in the absence of
others. There is certainly no active interpersonal relationship in such an experience, unless the person
could be laughing in response to his being alone—with
his being alone as the punch line of an interpersonal
joke. It is not necessary, however, to carry the matter to such lengths in order to discredit this apparent
objection of playing or joking by oneself. We need only
turn to the conventional concept of personality as being
composed of multiple personae. With this authority, we
understand that a man laughing alone in a room is engaged in intrapsychic "interpersonal" behavior. One
portion of his personality is joking with another portion.
That this is more than a matter of quibbling by definition is attested by the phenomena of imaginary companions in childhood play and "talking to oneself" and
the gross splitting of personality that takes place in
various pathologic conditions.

There are, of course, other areas in which humor and play overlap, besides the four presented above. It is beyond the modest aspirations of this book to go further in this particular phase of the examination. Enough has been presented to convince the reader of the soundness of the intuitive impression that relationship does exist between humor and play. Also, in the process of this examination, several topics have been approached which deserve more extensive development in their own right.

I shall review, at this point, some of the major phases of play and humor through which the developing human passes, with comment on smiling and laughter, play, riddles, adult humor, and slapstick. In the case of smiling and laughter, there are some particular difficulties associated with the period of early childhood. As mentioned already, some persons deny that young children ever enjoy humor, and hold that a child laughs a "joyful" rather than a "humorous" laugh or smiles a "warm" rather than a "mirthful" smile. To avoid becoming mired in this controversy, I shall attempt to stay on the firm ground of commenting on actual experiences or contexts in which the smile or laugh occurs, rather than try to ascribe the laugh to a playful mood or a humorous mood, or whatever. (The gold tile of our mosaic is brought to mind.)

Child psychologists instruct us that babies usually start smiling at about two or three months of age. It is interesting to note that this smiling activity occurs somewhat in advance of other important behavior— crawling, talking, controlling sphincter actions. On the other hand, the smile is, of course, preceded in onset by most of the vital biochemical body mechanisms. There are other emotional expressions also—such as rage or excitement—that might precede smiling. Adults are frequently surprised (and perhaps amused) by the sorts of things at which very young children smile or laugh. Infants may be stimulated to response by many things at which adults would find it difficult to laugh or

smile.   An infant may laugh at colors or shapes, or
at types of movement, or at parts of their own bodies.
An infant may smile at a sunbeam on the rug or a red
ball.   My second son was one day left by himself for a
few minutes in front of a department store mirror.   He
was seven months old.   Upon my wife's return to him,
she found the baby surrounded by an amused group of
people.   He was apparently unaware of the crowd and
was entertaining himself by looking in the mirror.   Each
time he looked up to see his mirrored image, he burst
into infectious laughter.   (A common element in these
experiences is the element of discovery--which element
some persons have described as a basic element of
humor.)

Play soon becomes the setting for many laughs and
smiles.   Playful acts whereby one cajoles an infant's
smiles are familiar to all—peekaboo, ride-a-cock-horse,
drop-the-baby, etc.   It is frequently during the process
of this play that the baby's first laugh occurs.   When
the intensity of the interaction is high enough, a smile
may spill over into articulation—and become a laugh.
The laugh appears to represent an advance of emotional
expression, from response involving facial muscles to
that involving respiratory, pectoral, and cervical muscles as well.   Paroxysm helps to distinguish laughter
from the many other sounds an infant makes.   Furthermore, laughter is allied by paroxysm with those other
paroxysmal phenomena—hiccough, sobbing, retching, orgasm, cough, and convulsions.

With such humble beginnings as a game of peekaboo, play grows to a great importance in human life.
Early, after infancy, the child's emphasis is on self-
contained play—in which the child prepares and presents to himself the fantasy he plays.   This emphasis
usually maintains a maximum between three and five
years of age.   The child frequently creates imaginary
companions to share in his enjoyment.   Fantasy and
creative imagination begin to exercise a major influence in the child's activities.

Play with other children establishes its supremacy during a later period—four to seven years. It would be a monumental task to determine the number of hours spent each day by children throughout the world playing cowboys and Indians, circus, pirates, house, mother and father, doctor, etc., etc. Fantasy is directed toward the relationships between people. Children take various roles, imagine various situations. The limits are those of human ingenuity. The interpersonal play of this older child is different from its earlier counterpart (peekaboo, etc.) and similar to its more contemporary counterpart (self-contained play), in that the child's own creative imagination is more actively involved. The fantasy is more the child's own creation and less that extended to him by his playmate. There are many complications in this comparison but, in brief, the child is more personally committed to the fantasy process.

This period also is marked by the onset of an interest in games (as distinct from play). We shall presently discuss games at greater length. Enough to say at this point that the interest in games increases from this period on, whereas the participation in play generally experiences gradual decrease from its maximum during these years.

Riddles—different from humor and play and yet also somewhat of a crossbreed of the two—attract considerable interest during the years five to eight. These riddles may seem primitive to the sophisticated adult— "When is a door not a door?"—but one would do well to remember the valuable tendencies that are given experience by these riddles. Riddles are, in one sense, early experiences of formalization of intellectual behavior. The riddle may be considered to be a parent to the anecdotal joke. Also, the riddle is quite obviously a playing together in the sense that a contest is joined wherein the child hopes to confound the wits of others. A conundrum is used instead of the imaginary pistol or bow and arrow. This creative fire of imaginative play is combined with intellectual functioning,

resulting in the development of pleasure. It is not surprising to find the child becoming interested at this
time in arithmetic, spelling, and theology. There is
during this period a broad endeavor on the part of the
child to formalize his experiences and to impose the
rule of his intellect over his internal and external environment.

Anecdotal jokes begin to interest the child at a
still later date—six to eight years. The onset of interest in funny stories is rather sudden. At one time,
a child is apparently unaffected by a joke—except perhaps politely. A short time later, days or weeks, he
has developed a lusty interest in "adult" humor. It is
tempting to consider this sharp transition as a matter
of language comprehension—that the difference between
apathy and amusement depends upon whether or not the
child understands the specific content of the joke. Or
it could be conjectured that this transition depends on
the affective impact on the child of the ideas presented
by the joke. The potentiality for amusement would thus
be linked with the child's glandular development. Beyond these, we can consider the transition to be related
to some combination of psychologic processes attaining
a critical level of maturation at this time. These processes involve the abstracting capacity of the human
organism—the capacity for dealing effectively with a
hierarchy of conceptualization—a learning capacity. It
is axiomatic that human life demands extensive use of
this abstracting capacity: everything in life finds some
position in the hierarchy of levels of abstraction; much
in life invokes various combinations of these levels.
There will be much more to say of this capacity in
later chapters.

Another significant item, slapstick, is closely related to riddles. Slapstick combines an amount of
abstraction with a quantity of ongoing interpersonal behavior. It is most appreciated during pre- and early-
adolescent years.

The casual thinker might be deceived into dismissing slapstick as presenting little of human value to recommend it for scholarly consideration. This perfunctory dismissal fails to give credit to the ancient lineage of slapstick. Egyptian tomb murals depict slapstick of those remote times. Slapstick played a role in the Greek theatre. Although classically divided into Comedy and Tragedy, the Greek theatre also had other components. Slapstick was presented, with other types of entertainment—i.e., acrobatics, feats of strength, magic, pantomime, juggling, dancing. "Dorian farce," "Megarean comedy," "Athenian old comedy," "Cyclops plays," "Phlyox comedy," the slapstick of modern burlesque—these have many common elements. The names and places are different, but many of the themes, situations, and characters are the same.

The specific productions of the ancient farces were improvised on several general themes; much of present-day burlesque comedy is improvisation and "ad lib." The farces introduced a variety of stock figures, several of them costumed with grotesque body padding and prominently exaggerated phallus. There is still "phallic" behavior in burlesque comedy. It has been largely sublimated into the oversize shoes, the rubber cane, the clown's bladder-balloon, and the "slapstick." Travesties of mythological stories lampooned both gods and men. The stock characters included caricatures of the gods—Zeus, Venus, Hera—and human character types—the old woman, the doctor, the slaves, the drunkard, the cook, the glutton, etc. Legendary heroes and heroines—Herakles, Odysseus, Oedipus, Priam, Helen—received a share of ridicule. In modern times, the lampooning of public heroes by the comedians of vaudeville and burlesque has produced familiar caricatures of Hitler, Churchill, Roosevelt, Mussolini, etc., etc.

There are only fragments of the scenarios of Greek farces available to us now, but many scenes are preserved on pottery and in statuary. The resemblance to modern slapstick comedy, and particularly burlesque, is striking. Clowns chase each other; there are struggles with "superior" inanimate objects; mock jealousies and disappointments, the techniques of exaggeration, the concentration on the physical aspects of humanity—all illustrating the generic ties of this ancient slapstick and its present-day counterpart.

Slapstick is largely interpersonal. Two clowns are throwing custard pies at each other. The episode involves a degree of symbolization, in that custard pies are used instead of fists. The interpersonal theme of the plot, however, is frankly presented. When the clowns both throw the pies at the same time or take turns at throwing the pies, an obviously symmetrical relationship exists. When the clowns divide up the interaction so that one is the "straight man," a complementary type of relationship develops. Interpersonal behavior, however, is the basic element. The resemblance in this between slapstick and play is marked. Crude, relatively simple symbols are used and the nature of interpersonal relationship is slightly obscured in both.

Frequently, the resemblance is so close that the mere addition of an audience will change "play" to "slapstick." Other types of slapstick—such as the episode wherein the clown struggles with an inanimate object—involve more complex symbolization both as to the content of the "joke" and as to the interpersonal foundation. A warmly remembered sequence is the Laurel and Hardy window-blind episode. Opening onto a stairway which the two comedians are frantically running up and down is a window with a window blind. Apparently the lock of the blind has worn out and the spring has become bewitched. The blind will not stay in the position desired and keeps rolling up and down— to the consternation of the ascending and descending comedians.

Although quite easily recognized as slapstick, this "joke" has little of the crudity of the custard pie. The themes of competition and struggle are active, whether they involve a custard-pie-throwing clown or a window blind. But other, more subtle elements are introduced.

A beautiful parallel is presented between the up-and-downness of the window blind and the up-and-downness of the comedians. The behavior of the window blind becomes a mute but eloquent comment on the relationship of the two comedians. One pulls the blind down; it rolls back up. The other pulls the blind down; it stays down for a few seconds, then rolls up again. The myriad of combinations is a testimony to the subtlety of the abstraction. Themes of personification of objects and objectification of persons can similarly be discovered in this "joke." With even a very superficial inspection of this particular joke, we can grasp some measure of the degree of complexity that may be found in slapstick. The complexities and subtleties of the abstractions involved in such slapstick items as the above may approach those of adult humor.

Throughout this survey—infant's play, the play of childhood, riddles, "jokes," slapstick—we can observe the vagueness and shiftiness of the line separating play and humor. Overlapping of the two is found in several areas. As mentioned previously, without some formal idea of specific differences between play and humor, one might find himself considering the two to be identical. It is as if, in the analogy of the mosaic, two tiles were set side-by-side closely resembling one another in shape and so similarly tinted that some scientific instrument would be needed to effect the differentiation. With such a relationship, these two tiles could appear to be twins, if set slightly apart in the matrix. Or, if placed contiguously, they could appear to be a single larger tile. But it would not be giving proper credit to the complexity of human psychology to embark on a program of establishing identity for these particular items of human life. The human organism is capable of preparing far greater subtlety than mosaic of identical tiles or a single ceramic sheet would indicate.

Review these four areas of overlap previously presented. (1) Nothing has been developed yet regarding the logical paradoxes found in both humor and play.

That development must await a later chapter. (2) Laughter and smiling are ascribed to both of our subjects. One is frequently hard put to identify each particular laugh as one signifying humor or as a laugh indicating playfulness. (3) In slapstick, infant's play, riddles, etc., are discovered varying degrees of overt interpersonal behavior. The implication carried by this discovery is, again, that humor and play overlap in this area. I shall attempt, as this book progresses, to increase an understanding of the role of interpersonal behavior in humor.

Even more difficult to discuss than the preceding is (4) the matter of spontaneity versus self-watchfulness. I have indicated, in the discussion of my uncomfortable statistical adventure of counting laughs and smiles, that the concept of levels of abstraction is central to this matter. Also, humor and play are quite sensitive to shifts in the spontaneity-thoughtfulness balance, and these two items of life might easily be discussed as activities wherein humans practice or even develop their skill at maintaining this balance. Implicit to the bringing together of these ideas is the belief that humor and play involve, in a way that is vital to the nature of both, manipulation of the levels of abstraction. It is my hope to present this belief more fully and more clearly as the book proceeds. During this presentation, an interesting fusion will be observed to take place between overlap areas 1 and 4. "Logical paradoxes" and "spontaneity self-watchfulness" will find a meeting ground in the concept of levels of abstraction.

There is a preliminary point about levels of abstraction that can be made at this time. This point has to do with a difference in the order of the levels of the abstractions involved in play as compared to the order of those involved in humor. The order of the levels of humor is found to be more complex than that of play. Humor presents a wider array of levels in a smaller unit than play. The shifts of the levels involved in humor are more rapid. Play is characterized by a simplicity and drawn-outness of its symbolic process. Consider the matter of the abstractions involved in the child-cowboy's play—"Bang! You're dead!" Each of these rather simple acts of abstraction serves as the basis for hours of elaboration, restatement, reinterpretation. An adult is soon exhausted by the repetitiveness of child's play. The symbolization remains the same. Play invokes a relatively simple symbolic process and depends, to a large extent, on sheer force of number for its impact.

The simplicity and directness of play are not found in the experiences of humor—neither in those jokes which are told by a joker to his audience nor in the "jokes" that set people to laughing about what has developed in their lives. We may use, as a talking example, the joke about the two psychiatrists who meet in the street. One greets the other: "You're fine. How am I?"

At times, this story will be found to be amusing. Let us list some variants that would likely fail to be amusing. (a) One psychiatrist could greet the other: "I'm fine. How are you?" (b) Two sheepherders meet in the street, and one greets the other: "You're fine. How am I?" (c) Two psychiatrists meet in the street and one greets the other: "You're sick. How am I?" (d) Two psychiatrists meet in the street and one greets the other: "I'm sick. How are you?" (e) Two psychiatrists meet in the street and exchange greetings. (f) Two psychiatrists meet in the street and exchange cards. There is another variant that might be somewhat amusing. It would probably have been much more amusing fifty years ago than it might be now. (g) Two doctors meet in the street and one greets the other: "You're fine. How am I?" Such an array (and others) of unhumorous variants could be compiled for any joke. I submit that the vastness of the number of such unhumorous variants bespeaks the subtlety of the symbolization process involved in an experience or a story that is really funny. We have, on one side, a large collection of variants which are not, or are only remotely, humorous. On the other side there is a quite small number

of actually amusing "jokes." It must be considered that
a rather high-powered selection factor is in operation.
The amusing joke must carry all those messages which
are implied by its unhumorous variants. In addition, it
must carry the more general statement of its own
punch line, and this in such a manner that the implicit
is not rudely exposed. Shifts in this complex collection of levels of abstraction are rapid; a punch line
delivers its punch in a space of seconds.

As contrasted to the repetitiousness of play, humor
loses much of its strength with repetition, either of the
same joke or by the telling of a series of jokes that
are too similar in nature. Humor and play seem to
have a comparison similar to that between a fine work
of art as contrasted with a child's fingerpainting.

A further comment on this comparison is available
in the more extensive consideration of games that was
promised several pages back. For the adult man or
woman, play is replaced to a large extent by sports
and games. Sports and games could be regarded as
play that has become organized, with definite goals and
purposes. A formality and underlying seriousness is
introduced with games and sports. (Play becomes a
game when it is played "for keeps.") There is a parallel in the fate of tickling. Tickling for the youngster
is hilarious play; for the adolescent and the adult, tickling becomes a stratagem of courtship.

Sports have their symbolization, to be sure. But
complex and rigid rules impose a new order that renders
quite obscure any relationship with the relatively un-
structured play of childhood. The referents for symbolization are forcefully repressed; the abstractions are
forced to greater complexity. The multitudes of rules
and the elaborate structures of sports or, say, a game
like chess, operate to complicate the fantasy. If a teen-
ager is angry with his father, it may give him considerable satisfaction to hit a baseball with a bat. He is
forever, however, throughout the game, forced to remember that it is a game of baseball, not Oedipus Rex,

One is given the impression that there is something curiously disruptive about play in adult games. There is little occasion for laughter in these games. The game is too serious. If laughter does occur, it is found to be an intrusion and the context of the game is violated. Such experiences are easily remembered, when a game of chess or a football contest has "degenerated" into playfulness, with resultant breaking of rules, laughter, and realigning of relationships. Brought to mind is the consternation in headquarters at the Christmas comradeship of the front-line German and Allied troops in World War I. The "game" of war was disrupted by this breach of the rules; the context had been shattered.

In recent years, attempts have been made to insert play into organized sports. We have the clowns who participate in swimming and diving matches, the exhibition slapstick that sometimes precedes a baseball game, the "horsing around" that frequently takes place between the halves of a football game. An unpredicted result is that these attempts actually underline the basic seriousness of sport (and games). The unhappy fate of present-day wrestling is a case in point. The addition of preposterous names, false curls, exaggerated grunts and grimaces has resulted in an activity that is no longer a sport. It has been stated that there is no such thing as professional wrestling in the United States. College wrestling, where such comedy relief has been avoided, remains as a completely different sort of phenomenon from the slapstick that is called professional wrestling.

Laughter is inserted with the result that it feels foreign to the sport, something extraneous added by patent outside manipulation. There is an awkwardness at the edge of the laughter. This awkwardness, in relief, emphasizes the rigidity of the game into which it has been inserted. One can help identify a diamond by scratching glass with it.

Much practice is needed for the development of the skill of maintaining a balance of spontaneity and thoughtfulness (or watchfulness, or detachment, as you may call it). Usually, this skill is quite adequate to the challenges that life offers to it. But, on certain occasions, such as my experiment, the techniques of balancing that one has developed may be discovered to be inadequate. The necessity is presented for renewed efforts. When such occasions arise, one is impressed—by the contrast with how easy things are ordinarily and by the intensity of the discomfort that now exists but was not there several moments before—with the degree of the skill otherwise taken for granted.

Participation in play and humor provides opportunity for practice with this balancing skill. Becoming skilled in playing or joking (or riddle telling or slapstick) provides one with a degree of skill in maintaining one's equilibrium of the two antithetical states—spontaneity and thoughtfulness. When balance is stable, the spontaneity of the ongoing process of life is not paralyzed by the detachment of thoughtfulness, or self-watchfulness is not lost in a hysteria of spontaneity.

It is relevant, from several contexts, to consider at this point the problem of the dedicated man. The dedicated man can be defined as a man who has been forced to achieve a balance of extremes in the spectrum of varying proportions of spontaneity and thoughtfulness. With a skill born of desperation, he develops capacity for inclusive restructuring of experience in terms of his idiosyncratic balance of much spontaneity and little self-watchfulness. The operation of this skill requires much effort and attention. One might invoke the principle of the lever as background. The shorter the arm of the lever with which one has to work, the more force one has to put into lifting the load into a position of equilibrium.

The dedicated man is efficient and frequently admired though considered deviant. (Leonardo was "inspired"; Napoleon was an "evil genius"; Blake was

touched with "divine madness.") With scarcely a moment's hesitation, he must, and is able to, meet each
moment of decision with an opinion that is so structured
as to allow him to persist in, depending on one's viewpoint, his inspiration or folly. "Dedication" lies in the
fact of his unswerving pursuit of a goal and an interest. It is not that the dedicated man has a moral or
philosophic objection to objectivity. There are those
who are dedicated to objectivity. Rather, it is a matter of his finely developed skill in blending thoughtfulness into the spontaneous, ongoing process of life so
that no jolts or discontinuity can exist. One might anticipate that my smile-laughter experiment would prove
to present considerable difficulty to a dedicated man,
but that, with his desperation-driven skill, he would be
able to restructure the experiment in such a way as to
preserve his characteristic spontaneity-thoughtfulness
balance, extreme though it is. All things are grist to
his mill. His stout techniques of harmonizing would
be adequate for protecting him from the uncomfortable
degree of self-awareness that grew upon me during the
period of experimental observation.

Paradoxically, an extreme comparable to the dedicated man's equation may be thought of as being represented by the fervent self-contemplation, or thoughtfulness, of the anchorite, whose life has become dedicated
entirely to the consideration of those thoughts and sensations that pass through his consciousness. The anchorite adopts an existence in which an "opinion about
the moment" has almost become the moment itself. He
achieves a product different from that of the dedicated
man, according to one interpretation. Viewed in a
larger sense, the product is the same. The anchorite's
exclusive thoughtfulness is indeed his own dedication.
Certainly the skill of the anchorite and that of the dedicated man are of the same family.

One is reminded of certain hypnotic techniques. If
an extraneous noise occurs near a hypnotic subject, it
can disrupt his trance, unless it is incorporated into
the trance instructions by the hypnotist. When so

incorporated, this otherwise disturbing noise can actually function to help the subject intensify the trance state. Similarly, a thought that might come to the subject as a disruptive influence can be incorporated and can offer a trance-reinforcing effect. The hypnotist might say, "And as you are becoming drowsy, certain thoughts may come to your mind that might make you sleepier and sleepier." That the capacity for developing the skill of the dedicated man or the anchorite is not foreign to the rest of humanity is argued for by the general ability to hypnotize oneself and by the dreamer's ability so to incorporate an external noise ("thoughtfulness" for the dedicated man, "spontaneity" for the anchorite) into his dream that the dream (or ongoing process of life) is not disrupted. An alarm clock ringing becomes the tolling of the church bell in the streets of the little Alpine town through which the sleeper wanders in his dream.

A danger exists that must be rendered inoffensive. In referring to "practice" ("Much practice is needed for the development of the skill of maintaining a balance"), an interpretation of behavior is considered that could imply disruption in the ongoing life process. To the extent that one practices at living, to that extent is one doing something more complicated than merely living. "Practice" invokes the very thoughtfulness that one practices to balance with spontaneity. And so one practices to blend practice into the equation. A structure similar to the Chinese egg puzzle is apparent. One egg lies within the other, larger or smaller, depending on which direction one is thinking, to the point where perception is exceeded and the series seems to end. But how can one be sure, if perception limits are exceeded, in either direction of magnitude, that there aren't other eggshells, unperceived, beyond these limits? And one is forced to contemplate the problem of the infinite series.

The danger lies in the paradox that to the extent that play or humor might be perceived as being "practiced at" by the participant, to that extent is his practice as wind on a desert. The anchorite, with his ongoing process of life consisting largely of thoughtfulness, conceives of himself as immersed in the life process—this is his mission, in this his life is with God and the Infinite. If one were to "practice at," rather than practice balancing spontaneity and objectivity, one would be denying the very process that one is practicing. Faced with this rather complicated concept, it is necessary to reaffirm one's recognition of the existence of various levels of abstraction. "Practice" and practice are rendered two vastly different phenomena by the implications of the punctuation.

This matter is more than one of punctuation or esoteric speculation. What is done to practice by rendering it as "practice," can also be done to many other aspects of life—such as, life and "life," humor and "humor," etc. When one "practices," one negates the practice. When one is "humorous," one destroys the humor.

CHAPTER II

Problems in Humor

Despite the widespread enthusiasm for humor and the general indulgence in the pleasure of it, despite humor's being one of the fundamental behavior patterns of the human organism—despite these signs of its importance and the recognition of that importance, many basic controversies still rage over it. Many of the most elementary questions concerning humor, smiling, and laughter remain unanswered.

These questions have been argued over for centuries; they have been rephrased, forgotten, and rediscovered, attacked from a wide variety of different approaches. Their discussion has involved the time and energies of many persons of high and low repute, in hallowed halls and barrooms. It is disappointing how many of them remain unanswered. To give some idea of the scope of the difficulty and to demonstrate the depth of the obscurity, I shall survey some of these controversial areas here, with no attempt at this point to answer any of the questions presented.

First, there is a question already touched upon. Are smiling and laughing manifestations of the same process? Or do they represent different entities entirely? It is argued that smiling and laughing are obviously different acts which involve different musculature, different nerves, different brain centers. They look different and sound different. They appear under somewhat different conditions. On the other hand, it is contended that these differences dwell on superficialities and that, excluding the ironic smile, the sardonic laugh, and the like, smiling and laughter are associated with the same emotional process.

Second, there is the question of "What is it that makes people laugh?" This is also phrased "Why do people laugh?" or "How does something funny make a person laugh?" A related question is "What is the nature of humor?" or "Why is a joke (or anything else) funny?" All of these questions are concerned with a curiosity about the process whereby something perceived by us sets up an internal reaction which is described by ourselves as amusement and which results in the outward manifestations of smiling and laughing. Attempts have been made to examine this process from a large number of philosophic, psychologic, and metaphysic viewpoints. These examinations have generally served to increase the confusion.

Certainly this is an important family of questions. Not merely concerned with classifying or describing, they inquire about humor and man himself. Philosophically, one could project an item of humor existent alone, without the human beings to be amused by it—somewhat like the Berkeleian forest projected in dealing with the philosophic question of whether a tree makes a sound as it falls in that forest if no mortal is there to hear it fall. Our curiosity, however, demands mortal presence for this question on humor and we generally refuse to tackle the problem of conceiving of a laugh "untouched by human lips." And so these questions ask both about some vague abstract called humor and also about that plump man—the prototype of all his fellows—sitting over there in the corner, howling with laughter, holding his sides, tears running down his cheeks.

Another as yet unsettled question is "Why is amusement pleasant?" Or, using other words, "What is there about a smile that makes it an enjoyable experience for

people?" There is no question that smiling and laughing are desirable activities for most people. (A small
number of people suffering with pathologic conditions
actually do avoid these activities because of their unpleasant effects.) Most of us feel pleasure when we
are amused, and remember those moments as happy
ones. But we are not yet able to say why this is so.

The controversy about the baby's smile continues.
Some persons say that it is an imitative action, a first
social response to the presence of a fellow human.
There are others who feel that it may be imitative,
but not necessarily social. Some hold it to be a social
response, but not imitative. And there are some icono-
clasts who feel that it is not social, not imitative, but
some sort of belch.

The curious business of cartoons has aroused much
interest. Cartoons have been with us for many years.
The cartoon is an important subtype of the general
category that is named, in this book, canned jokes. It
represents an artificial creation, apparently not directed
to our own lives, but which touches us in a very personal way.
    The production of cartoons is an elaborate art.
There are many people who subsist entirely by their
skill at this art. This skill is occasionally carried
to the point that some cartoons seem to result in a
total suspension of physical rules; there occurs a very
peculiar holiday from entropy, the mills of the gods,
and so on. These cartoons are self-contained and do
not require a beginning or an end. They are the story,
the build-up, and the punch line all in one. One such
cartoon is the skier cartoon of Charles Addams, showing two ski tracks trailing down the snow-covered hill,
dividing around a sturdy tree—one on one side, the
other on the other side—and again uniting as a pair to
continue down the hill together. The skier who apparently accomplished this odd feat is himself pictured,
intact, still with both skis attached at the end of the

long run. Such cartoons as this are rare and are considered great art by many persons. The spectacle of such contrived articles as cartoons amusing such a large number of otherwise reasonable persons is a fascinating and puzzling one. Several groups of psychologists have experimented with using cartoons as projective devices in personality assessment—on the very basis that puzzles us, that cartoons have an intimate appeal and touch us deeply within our psychic beings.

Do animals have a sense of humor? This is another question that has received much attention in the past, and which is still unresolved. Two opposing views are presented. One holds that animals do experience amusement, that they do smile when amused, and that they even laugh occasionally. Instances are presented of apes grinning in a manner suggestive of the human smile. It is also held that in appropriate situations they demonstrate behavior which resembles different types of human laughter behavior. Other animals—dogs, cats, horses, hyenas, lions, and others—have been variously discussed as smilers or laughers. On the other hand, a large number of those persons who have concerned themselves with this matter subscribe to the view that animals do not smile, do not laugh, and are never amused.

Another problem is found in the consideration of the evolution of amusement sources in each person's life. "Why does play become a game which becomes a riddle which becomes a joke?" What process of maturation is there in the human organism which results in the transition from play to game to riddle and then to joke? Children do not get the humor from jokes that adults do, and adults do not get the amusement from play that children do? Why is this? What psychologic process does this depend on? An associated question has to do with the structure of adult games. Most adult games—sports, theatricals,

card games, Scrabble, mah-jongg, etc.—have elaborate
and rigid rules for playing. There is not the undisci-
plined fantasy-production of children in these games.
Take chess, for instance. Fantasy underlies the whole
situation. And a game of chess is framed in the context
"this is a game of chess." But this fantasy is very
deep and the frame is implicit. One does not say to
one's chess partner, "You be my lover and we shall play
together." (Children do, however say, "You be the mother
and I'll be the father.") Ostensibly, in chess, two mature persons manipulate small carved pieces on a board,
according to rules, legends, precedents. The unconscious content—or fantasy—generally remains unconscious. Despite, or perhaps because of, all these rules
and this repression of fantasy, adults enjoy chess and
other games. They do not, however, burst into laughter
regularly during games; they do not describe their genuine enjoyment as amusement; they do not find, to return to our example, chess to be humorous. (Granted
that there are certain exceptions to this.)

Nevertheless, and here is where the puzzler enters,
there are certain times in the progress of an adult game
when, to the participants, the whole thing can become intensely amusing. Most frequently, this moment appears
at the end of the game. Occasionally, it takes place
during the game action itself. There is no mistaking this
sudden transition. Spectators are well aware that something different has happened and sometimes are irritated
by the change. The adult game is disrupted by this
hilarity. The question is then, what happens in a serious, well-disciplined game, which is not ordinarily a
source of humor, to result in these moments of amusement. What happens to produce this amusement?

Another difficulty, which Gregory Bateson suggested
as related to the above question, is presented in the
phenomenon of "laughing in church." This phenomenon
is the prototype of a large number of situations during
which laughter (or giggling, etc.) inappropriately appears.
From all external appearances, these situations are not,
nor could be conceived of as humorous. They are not,

in any easily determined manner, anything like the adult games discussed above. And yet, incongruously, laughter occasionally bursts out. Laughing in church is but one example. Laughter during weddings, graduation exercises, recitals, classroom recitations, speeches—and many other such instances—are familiar examples. Why are people prompted to laughter, from where do they derive their amusement during such procedures?

A field which has received attention and stimulated conflicting ideas is that concerning the relationship between the persons mutually involved in humor. What is the relationship between the persons smiling or laughing together? It has been suggested that humor embodies an attack by one individual on another. Laughter is then variously explained as resulting from feelings of superiority in attack or again as representing a compensatory reaction to feelings of inferiority in battle. On the other hand, some state that people can only smile and laugh together if they are feeling a deep love or affection for each other. Humor then seems to become a reaffirmation of "warm," "positive" emotions. It is also presented that persons mutually involved in humor are convertly indulging in some illicit, forbidden behavior. This behavior is usually represented as being of a sexual nature. And there are other ideas about this interpersonal relationship, none of which have been demonstrated to be conclusive.

Why cannot a person tickle himself? When another person tickles someone, the one tickled will frequently be amused and laugh. This is especially true of children and of young couples in love. But when you try to tickle yourself, it is not funny. It usually hurts. Why? You are touching the same place and doing the same thing to it. There are many other unanswered questions about tickling. Why do children get more fun from being tickled than adults? Why are certain areas of the body more sensitive to tickling than others. What is there about being tickled that produces laughter? Why does being tickled produce more laughter at certain times than at others?

Then there are the problems related to joke telling. Why does a joke seem less humorous when you <u>hear</u> it the second time, whereas you can <u>tell</u> some jokes over and over without experiencing any decrease in the fun of telling them? What about joke orgies? All of us can recall our participation at certain parties or gatherings where many jokes were told in an almost frenzied manner with much hilarity. The pitch of the whole session was high and the tempo increased. What produces such a frantic state?

And why does it improve the joke to tell it in dialect? Take the Maroony joke. Told in Irish dialect, it can be funny.

A policeman is pacing his beat in ol' Dublin when who does he see standing there on top o' that tall building but his friend Maroony. He wildly calls out, "Maroony, Maroony, don't jump! For the sake of yer mither, don't jump!"

Maroony answers, "To hell with me mither."

"Well, thin, Maroony, don't jump. For the sake of yer wife Bridget don't jump."

"To hell with me wife Bridget."

"Maroony, Maroony, for the sake of the Virgin Mary, don't jump."

"To hell with the Virgin Mary."

"All right, thin, jump, ye Protestant heathin!"

As written in straight English, the joke becomes strained. The dialect is thus seen as an important element of the joke.

There are also the questions associated with joke-presenting technique. (1) For the presenter to laugh occasionally and to be mildly amused by his own joke increases the power of its humor. For the presenter to laugh immoderately and to be obviously carried away by his own joke spoils the joke for the recipient. Why? (2) The joke must be understood as being a joke for it to be funny. Many practical jokes result in anger, fear, sadness—all sorts of inappropriate emotions—until the joke angle is revealed. Then the possibility of laughter becomes available. The implicit statement that "This is a joke" is of vital importance. What is its function? How does it work? (3) Another difficulty associated with technique concerns the manner of the joke presenter. Certain gestures, facial expressions, etc., enhance the humor of a joke. Certain types of behavior decrease the humor. Why? What are the ways in which these behavior types operate?

Certain mechanisms of joke structure are especially conducive to laughter. The joke with a series is an example of one such mechanism. The joke utilizing this structure device goes through a progressive series of steps—either with numbers, people, situations, or actions—before the punch line is finally reached. Example: A young man walks into a liquor store and asks the hard-bitten old clerk for a bottle of gin. The clerk thinks he sees an opportunity to have some fun, and so he asks, "Well, what kind of gin, young fellow? We have three kinds, you know. There is oxygin, hydrogin, and nitrogin." The customer is not as unsophisticated as all that, so he thinks a minute and then answers, "Oh, is that so? Very interesting. I didn't know that before. It's strange how things come in threes. Musturd, custurd, and you, you basturd." Why does this sort of structure increase amusement?

Another puzzling mystery is that of the "k" sound. It is legend among professional funnymen that this sound is itself enough to send people into gales of laughter. And, oddly enough, there is evidence to support the legend. What psychologic process is involved in this phenomenon?

The punch line[1] of a joke is a highly specialized article. It frequently presents a seemingly irrelevant

---

[1]"Punch line" is a fairly popular term and is used by me in a manner roughly approximating its popular use. I must request some reader indulgence concerning my use of the word, however, for in designating a humor climax, "punch line" will sometimes indicate an action or an attitude rather than an actual verbal "line."

idea, or it may seem incongruous with respect to the main body of the joke. Or it may seem to open up an entirely new trend of thought. Or the punch line may be an unexpectedly rational statement. As in the joke about the mama's boy. This fellow was about thirty-five years old when he finally decided that he would have to start thinking about going out on his own, leaving his mother. So, to prepare himself for this ordeal, he started psychoanalytic treatments. After three or four years of treatment he came bursting into his mother's room one day on his return from the analyst: "Oh, mama! We know what's wrong with me now. I've got an Oedipus complex!" Mama took another bon-bon from the box and said lazily, "Oedipus, smedipus, as long as you love your mama." What does the punch line need to be funny? Why do some structures amuse and others fail?

Finally, there are the relatively uninvestigated questions about humor, laughter, and smiling in various types of pathologic conditions. Excessive elation, amounting to hypomania or mania, is one of the major symptoms of the manic-depressive psychoses. Smiling and laughter and the appreciation of humor are altered in a variety of ways in schizophrenic psychoses. Not only are the causes of these alterations poorly understood, there is also great controversy as to the nature of the changes. Some psychiatrists assert that persons suffering with schizophrenia do not experience amusement, that they do not smile or laugh, that they do not understand jokes and cannot tell jokes. Other psychiatrists cannot agree. They have observed smiling and laughing (not of the "elation variety") in numerous persons suffering with schizophrenia. They have been told jokes by patients classified as schizophrenic. Undeniably, there is frequently a distinctive quality to the joke-presenting situation; there is frequently a somewhat different nature about the smile or laugh of the patient. There is much that needs to be understood about these clinical impressions.

The problem of cataplexy is another fascinating one.   This condition is a disease reaction whereby a person, under certain emotionally stimulating circumstances, is seized with a sudden weakness of the voluntary (skeletal) muscles of the body.   The emotions associated with this reaction may be those of surprise, fear, anger, joy, sadness, and—or—amusement.   Certain of these patients have found it necessary to go through life stifling all tendencies to laugh, avoiding humor, controlling all smiles.   They have found that if they are unexpectedly stimulated to laughter, their muscles may suddenly grow weak and they may collapse.   Their strength is then not available to them for variable lengths of time, ranging up to several minutes.   Because of the nonvital distribution of the muscles involved, this condition is rarely fatal, but it frequently proves to be quite bothersome and embarrassing.   These experiences apparently cause some internal changes which are as yet poorly understood, and result in an unbalancing of the body's homeostasis.

In addition, there are other pathologic conditions, usually associated with electrochemical and structural changes in the brain tissue, that have as one of their outward manifestations abnormality of humor mechanisms.   Patients suffering with pseudobulbar palsy, multiple sclerosis, Parkinson's disease, amyotrophic lateral sclerosis, cerebral arteriosclerosis, and brain tumors have all been described as being subject in one case or another to inappropriate and uncontrollable spells of laughter.   Many patients describe these spells as undesirable and unpleasant.   The spells have come to be called "sham mirth."   The fact remains that they have the outward appearance of true laughter and frequently appear in response to just those stimuli which, in the normal individual, will cause true laughter to appear.

For example, I told the following joke to an acquaintance suffering with one of these organic illnesses: A man walked into a bar and ordered a drink.   The bartender had just finished pouring the drink when he noticed, to his amazement, that the man had a green

onion tucked behind each ear. The bartender was a
discreet man and so said nothing about this peculiar
phenomenon. But the customer lingered on, and finally
the bartender could stand it no longer. He asked,
"Did you know that you've got a couple of onions behind your ears?" The man answered, "Yes—they are
just my color, aren't they?" My acquaintance broke
into a grin and made a short gasping noise in his
throat. I questioned him about his sensations. He
stated that, at the time of the punch line of the joke,
he experienced a very uncomfortable sensation similar
to an ache.

Some neurologists feel that the explanation for these
peculiar attacks has to do with the location in the brain
of the disease damage. Others have shown, however,
that quite a variety of brain sites are affected in such
cases. They believe that there is nothing specific
about the localization of humor centers in the brain.
This confusion remains without solution.

There are also people who are subject to fits of
laughter. The laughter is started in some such cases
by generally appropriate stimuli but continues, out of
control, beyond a normal time-span and may merge
into a generalized convulsive seizure. Or the laughing
fit may be punctuated by episodes of petit mal (brief
spells of unconsciousness) or terminate in psychomotor
fits (seizures of uncontrollable, bizarre behavior). The
laughing fits may be associated with spontaneous orgasm,
urination, or paresthesias and occasionally be accompanied by loss of consciousness after which a convulsive seizure which may develop. The laughter itself
is variously described as normal or exaggerated, as
soft or loud and barking. It may or may not be associated with feelings of amusement. The tendency to
these fits is frequently reduced by the same sorts of
treatments that alleviate idiopathic epilepsy. As a
matter of fact, it is proposed that they represent a
form of epilepsy, or that they are aurae (premonitory
episodes) for epileptic seizures. But it is difficult to
come to definite conclusions about them, to determine

what they represent with regard to the person's normal humor responses. And it is not known how laughter happens to be involved in such convulsive behavior.

The foregoing are some of the problems which puzzle those who contemplate humor. These problems are unsolved. At least, for every person who asserts that he has found the answer to any one of them, there seem to be many more who deny it. The purpose of this book is to bring together information made available by studies and research in several fields—such as medicine, biology, psychology, ethnology, religion, and philosophy—and apply these findings to humor. An attempt is made in the following chapters to bring together data and ideas that will indicate some answers to various ones of the questions asked above. As has been indicated, what follows is broadly structured into two parts. The loosely connected chapters of the next section provide discussion of several aspects of humor from a variety of rather divergent points of view. The two chapters of the concluding section are more of an integrated whole. They sketch the development of a theory of the structure of humor that has its debut in this book.

PART TWO

CHAPTER III

A Metaphoric Discussion

A brief discussion of some aspects of metaphor is pertinent at this point. Metaphor has particular value for the type of exposition used in this book. By this device, one is able to treat a psychologic phenomenon—in this case, humor—as a concrete object. In addition, the use of metaphor makes it possible to gather together items of humor—wit, comedy, slapstick, etc.—into a circumscribed object for contemplation. Finally, one also has the opportunity of arbitrarily choosing some particular characteristics of humor and, using them as the measure, dividing humor into a finite number of convenient segments.

For certain purposes of this book humor is arbitrarily divided into three segments. They are called canned jokes, situation jokes, and practical jokes. The first category, canned jokes, includes those jokes that are told or presented with little obvious relationship to the ongoing human interaction—humor which, on the surface, does not seem to find its origin in the ongoing process. Situation jokes are those which do find, to a major extent, their origin in the ongoing life process. In connection with this type of joking, words like "spontaneous" and "life" come to mind. Finally, practical jokes combine many features of the other two types, but are, nevertheless, distinctly different. The practical joke is a hybrid—both contrived and spontaneous.

In naming this category I am using a popular terminology and, as far as I can tell, my judgment of the jokes that I have put into this category matches quite well the general, popular concept of jokes which are "practical jokes."

As I have said, metaphorizing has certain definite advantages for exposition. These advantages are not obscure, and most readers are quite familiar with the metaphysical procedure as is here outlined. But be aware of the possibility of a serious danger in this device. The danger lies in what the science of general semantics calls map-territory problems. It is important to remember that naming a segment of humor experiences by the phrase "canned jokes" does not really tell us of what that piece consists—and similarly for "situation jokes" and "practical jokes." These labels are just that: they are the labels, not the humor or the specific jokes that are included in each category of humor.

It is seductively easy to speak of an item of humor as being a canned joke, without further comment. But in the end we would find ourselves even more confused than if each joke were individually presented and no attempt were made to categorize their multitude into a more easily managed structure. There would be canned jokes, situation jokes, and practical jokes—and zubladrils and squerches and hlrubfs—and we really would not have anything at all, because we would not know what on earth we were talking about. We might find ourselves in that tortured state of mind endemic to the advertising world where people talk on and on about products that are deprived of any real existence by the very things that advertising people say about them.

Consequently, the privilege of using a metaphoric device in exposition may carry with it the responsibility of defining rather extensively the crucial terms. It is not sufficient to say, "Oh, yes, canned jokes—you know what they are. They are the jokes that fall into one of the three categories of humor I have set up.

They are the 'canned jokes.'" From that sort of statement, for all we know, canned jokes could be anything from canned jokes to jokes in a can. This would obviously be a pretty ridiculous situation. And so defining the terms becomes an important activity.

At the opening of this chapter mention is made of having chosen "some particular characteristics of humor" as the measure whereby jokes would be classified as one or another of the three indicated types. We need, with reference to the map-territory problem, some clarification of the particular characteristics utilized. If these characteristics constitute the measure whereby humor items are categorized, it is an obligation to present a discussion of the characteristics.

There are, of course, many ways in which humor could be classified. It could be classified in terms of motive, or by the amount of resulting laughter. It could be categorized according to dialect, or according to the means of presentation—verbal, written, pictorial, lyric, verse, etc.—and in many other ways. One is under no general compulsion to categorize in one way or the other. I have chosen to classify according to a schema that is particularly useful from the standpoint of the type of ideas about humor I hope to have presented by the conclusion of this book. This is a purely arbitrary schema geared to the needs of the book, rather than to any beliefs about basic importance or cosmic values.

Canned jokes are defined as those which are presented with little obvious relationship to the ongoing human interaction. Situation jokes are indicated as those which are spontaneous and have, to a major extent, their origin in the ongoing interpersonal (or intrapersonal) process. The practical joke category is defined as that made up of jokes which are both presented and spontaneous—in that the joker consciously contrives his joke, but must depend on the unfolding of an interpersonal (or intrapersonal) process for the presentation of his joke.

These definitions emphasize several factors. Foremost, we find that emphasis is placed on the concept of humor as something that is communicated. And in this sense, humor is indicated as a mode of communication.

Communication is introduced as it is used in the phrase "communication theory,"—the study of the intra- and interpersonal web of exchange that binds all persons, one with the other. Communication theory considers all forms of command and information exchange as "communication." According to this theory, there are four levels on which communication takes place. There is the intrapsychic level where communication is known as feeling or thinking. Expanding outward, there are interpersonal communication between two individuals, group communication among members of a defined group, and mass communication among vaguely defined individuals in a large population. Communication is omnipresent and protean. There is internal communication as well as external, nonverbal communication as well as verbal, and also meta-communication, or communication about communication (codifying information, etc.), among all the rest. To be strictly accurate, one would say that communication theory concerns all that by which a nervous system might be influenced, in the sense that all neuronal events have a commanding and informative aspect. It is beyond the scope of this book to present a more extensive discussion on communication theory. The interested reader is referred to Bibliography items: 8, 35, 90, and 93.

Humor serves a myriad of communicative functions. Several of these functions have already received comment. Many others of these functions will appear during the unfolding of chapters further on. Some of these communication functions will be incorporated in the diagram of the structure of Humor, developed in the final section of the book. Suffice it to say at this point that the communication function of humor is emphasized in the schema of this book.

An important area that is emphasized in the definitions used to divide humor has to do with matters usually considered under headings such as "the unconscious" and "explicit versus implicit." We could suggest a slogan for this family of concepts—"There is more than meets the eye." The emphasis for these concepts is found in the definition words "interpersonal," "intrapersonal," and "obvious" (taken from the definition of a canned joke—"with little obvious relationship to the ongoing human interaction"). "Interpersonal" and "intrapersonal" events are widely recognized as having significant unconscious and implicit aspects. By the use of the word "obvious" in the definition of canned jokes I have attempted to indicate that, with these jokes also, the unconscious and the implicit may be significantly involved.

This area of emphasis certainly requires further exposition. Easier said than done! For one is faced with the difficulty of speaking of what is unspeakable by definition. Once the implicit is discussed, it is no longer implicit, but becomes explicit; unconscious content cannot be discussed unless it is no longer unconscious; and so on. The effort is rather like trying to shine a light on the blackness of the night to see it more clearly. Within the limitations of this difficulty, however, let us direct our attention to these two entities—the unconscious and the implicit.

A general commentary on the ubiquitous operation of the unconscious in humor is presented in the chapter immediately following this one. In that chapter, it is emphasized that all humor has implicit unconscious aspects—that each joke has, in its essence, a host of unconscious chords sounding in the audience mind no less loudly than does the explicit joke. I express my agreement with the Freudian position that these unconscious chords constitute a vital part of the humor structure.

At this point, we are ready to focus more specifically on the implicit. And, to begin our consideration, I must indicate that it may be peculiarly artificial to separate the unconscious and the implicit. Unconscious content—of humor, at least—is always, in a sense, also implicit content. The sense in which this is true has to do with the fact emphasized in Chapter IV that the unconscious content of a communication (I again use the word in its broader meaning) is, though not consciously expressed or realized, nevertheless an integral part of the essence or being of the communication.

Despite the artificiality of such a maneuver—i.e., setting the unconscious and the implicit as distinct one from the other—there is some tentative justification in nature for such an operation. In avoiding the sticky question of how unconscious the unconscious may be, we can settle on the point that there is implicit content of communication—such as a joke—other than the implicit unconscious content. By way of clarification, consider a joke.

A man finds himself ailing and seeks medical advice. He is instructed by his doctor that he suffers from a dangerous kidney ailment and must have a diet of mother's milk for the next six weeks if he is to continue his existence. The patient is very impressed by the doctor's statements and starts home, terribly concerned over the gravity of his condition and no less worried over the problem of where he will find a supply of mother's milk. He arrives at his apartment house, only to find his wife missing from their apartment. He steps across the hall with the thought that she might be visiting in the neighboring apartment, but the neighbor lady informs him that his wife is not there. And, chatting, she asks him about the results of the visit to the doctor's office. He informs the neighbor of his condition and speaks of the doctor's prescription, expressing his feelings of hopelessness about ever finding a handy source of mother's milk. But the neighbor lady hastily reminds him that she has recently delivered a baby and, it just so happens, has a generous abundance of mother's milk. She offers him a trial of her milk there and then. So the two of them settle down in the neighbor's apartment, she bares a breast, and the patient begins to nurse, according to the doctor's orders. After several minutes, the neighbor lady finds that this experience has some unexpectedly stimulating aspects and begins to move nervously about on her chair. She then asks hospitably if the patient would like anything else. But he doesn't respond, continues to nurse. As time passes, she becomes more and more aroused by the experience and suggests that the man might like something else to go along with his treatment and that she will be glad to provide it. No response; the nursing continues. Finally, she has become greatly aroused, is moving about on her chair with great ardor, and feverishly proclaims that she will be happy to give the man anything he might desire. At this he stops nursing, looks up at her, and asks, "Yuh got a cookie?"

Many themes suggest themselves as implicit to the explicit content of this joke. "Sick people become childlike" may be one such. Or, "Mother's milk is lifegiving." Or, "Business before pleasure." There may be many other implicit themes that are also unconscious. A possible unconscious theme implicit in this cookie joke might have to do with the Oedipus theme and the taboo against incest, with the beneficent neighbor lady representing a seductive mother and the sick man here representing an ill-advised and incestuous son. Such unconscious themes as this are of a different order of things from the examples of implicit information given above, such as "Business before pleasure." Unconscious content is unconscious for a reason, and has intimate, personal meaning for each of us. This is not true of implicit content that is implicit merely because of the fact that it has been suggested but not explicitly stated. There is no deep personal truth in the merely implicit, as there is in that information that is both implicit and unconscious. In the last analysis, the difficulty boils down to a matter of definition. All information that is not explicit is implicit. And there is both the "merely" implicit and the "unconscious" implicit. Finally, in a crude way of speaking, the merely implicit is overt content, whereas

the unconscious implicit is that which is covert, private,
and usually inaccessible.   One can readily call forth
the merely implicit; it is extremely difficult to beguile
the unconscious implicit.

Having brought affairs to a comfortable state of
understanding, things will now be stirred up again by
introducing the concept of levels of abstraction, as it
applies to any implicit-explicit dichotomy.   We are
faced with the discovery, here, that the two (explicit
and implicit) are on different levels of abstraction—in
that the implicit is by definition a commentary on the
explicit.   An explicit communication—nonverbal, such
as pointing the direction to a traveler, or verbal, such
as the joke recounted above—is put forth as an article
of exchange.   With each such explicit communication
are clustered various other implicit communications.
In the case of the cookie joke, there are "Sick people
become childlike," or "Mother's milk is life-giving,"
the Oedipus theme, etc.   These implicit themes are
comments upon the explicit content of the joke.   And in
this same sense, these implicit themes are located on
different levels of abstraction from the explicit joke
content.   ("Levels of abstraction" applies similarly to
both the merely implicit and the unconscious implicit.)
   It's the case of the picture of the girl on the old
familiar Dutch Cleanser can, who was pictured holding
a can of Dutch Cleanser on which was pictured a girl
holding a can of Dutch Cleanser on which was pictured
a girl holding a can of Dutch Cleanser, ad infinitum.
If we set up a hierarchy of abstraction—ranging up from
the most concrete to the most abstract—we seem to
find at the beginning of the hierarchy the can of cleans-
ing powder which can be picked up and felt, tossed
about, and used in house cleaning.   That can has on its
label a picture of a girl holding a can.   The picture,
as a picture of the object-can, is on a next higher level
of abstraction.   And then there is the picture on the
can in the picture on the object-can.   This picture, in
its context of being a picture of a picture on a can, is

on yet another, higher level of abstraction. And so on and on, into the endless tail of the infinite regress.

In the case of the joke, the explicit joke content is, on first glance, at the bottom of the ladder and represents the object level that seems to be represented also by the actual Dutch Cleanser can. The explicit story about the man with the kidney ailment who needed mother's milk is apparently the equivalent of the object can and may be the beginning of a hierarchical climb from "most" concrete to "most" abstract. There is then, on a next higher level, the implicit information that is communicated about the joke content—"Sick people become childish," etc. These implicit communications are formulated on the basis of the explicit joke content. Once we have made the initial step off the ground, other implicit statements become admissible. " 'Sick people become childish,' is an implicit statement communicated by the joke about the man with the kidney ailment" would be one example of these higher-level statements. On a yet higher level would be the statement, "Jokes contain implicit statements, is indicated by the information that 'sick people become childish' is an implicit statement communicated by the joke about the man with the kidney ailment." I am sure that it is not necessary to pursue this sort of thing further. The series is endless.

Before going further in this adventure, it might be refreshing and informative to make use of the opportunity to play a mental game. Return to the so-called object level and reverse direction of march, so to speak. We can demonstrate to ourselves that the joke is not a "most concrete" object. The joke may be seen as an abstraction of some portion of the ongoing life process. The joke, which was initially taken for the "most concrete," can be considered as not the "most concrete," but rather as an abstraction embodying implicit communication about a more fundamental "thing"—i.e., the ongoing life experiences obtaining at the time.

Pursuing this game even further, we can carry on this sort of nihilistic reverse marching to the point of

questioning the substantiality of the Dutch Cleanser can
as an object. In the context of certain sorts of explanation, the can is no object, but rather a specific concentration of molecules. The molecules, according to
our modern theories of physics, are existent as specific concentrations of smaller particles which, in their
turn, are existent as specific concentrations of something vaguely known as energy.

This questioning could extend in a like fashion to
the "ongoing life process" mentioned above as being on
the next less abstract level from the joke; it could be
argued that this "life process" is an abstraction of the
cellular events taking place in the bodies of the participants in the life process. Further, these so-called
cellular events could be described as abstractions for
behavior of molecules, which molecules are considered
existent as specific concentrations of smaller particles,
and so on.

When the game is carried out to its logical conclusion, we are faced with the strange prospect of arguing
for the absence of an absolute concreteness at any level
higher than that of basic energy. And who on earth
really knows what energy is? We write "energy equals
ML^2T^{-2}" ($E = ML^2T^{-2}$). That should help to fix the
Cheshire Cat. But we are foiled by the knowledge
that after all, mathematical symbolization (such as
$E = ML^2T^{-2}$) represents, in many ways, the crowning
glory of the abstracting ability of the human brain.
Where is objective "reality"? Perhaps we all are a
bit more vaporous than ordinarily supposed. That we
might be less solid, or concrete, would certainly make
more easily explainable such interesting phenomena as
the passage of a spear through flesh or electron streams
through steel or light waves through glass. In the last
analysis, everything in the world boils down to concentration of energy. And, again, who knows what energy
is? Can you feel it? Can you sit down on it? Can
you contain water within it? Well, yes—in a rather
abstract way. $E = ML^2T^{-2}$! In the context of this
mental game, this formula illustrates the paradox that

the "most concrete"—that is, energy—is conceivable to human brains only in terms of a "most abstract"—that is, a theoretic concept.

Such nihilistic considerations as the above are really beyond the scope of a book on humor. They are included to help set for the reader the general mood of the philosophies of this book. Practically, items found on some less ultimate level than energy must be treated as the "object" or "thing" at the concrete end of the levels-of-abstraction hierarchy. We must agree on a more practical "objective reality." Since we are human and since what we know best is that which impinges on the "sensory organ" of the human brain, the so-called ongoing life processes have top priority in the choice of a practical concretion. So then, arbitrarily taking the ongoing life process as the objective reality, we return to the concept that the joke is a comment on that "life process" and is one level higher on the ladder of abstraction (besides being part of that "life process" reality).

What happens when this "level" concept is applied in a study of jokes. In terms of the schema used to categorize humor, those items of behavior called practical jokes are seen most easily as multilevel phenomena.

To the practical joker and the observers (not to the joke-victim) it is known that what is happening is a joke. They know that "there is more than meets the eye." In other words, what is happening—for example, the joke-victim is reaching for an apparently abandoned purse—seems to be happening. The joke-victim bends down! He is reaching for the purse! Explicit content. Real life. But, it is not really that way—because it is a joke. The joker and the observers know this. The recognition of this episode (which is unfolding itself before their eyes, in such a "real life" way) as a joke is part of the mentality of these jokers and observers.

The joke-victim, however, seems to be operating in a different sort of system. He is engaged in a "real

life" episode of picking up an abandoned purse. He
does not see the string tied to the purse; he does not
know that the joker is over there behind the fence,
ready to yank the purse away as soon as the victim
stoops to seize the prize. The recognition of the episode as a joke is not available to the victim. The
purse is a purse lost in the street. He bends over to
pick it up and discover the treasures inside.[1]

In summary, there are the ongoing life process (a
man is stooping to pick up a seemingly abandoned purse,
and a joker and the observers are participating in a
practical joke with an unwitting joke-victim) and the
joke ("there's more than meets the eye"). They are,
in a sense, one and the same. They are, in another
sense, two different "things." In that sense, the joke
is an abstraction of the so-called life process. The
joke becomes a next-level-up comment on the life
process (and thus, on itself as part of that life process).

The multilevel concept applies as well to situation
and canned jokes. In the instance of situation jokes,
the definition states they find their origin in the ongoing
life process. The "ongoing life process" is accompanied
by many "unconscious implicit" and "merely implicit"
themes. We have found ample evidence for this belief
in preceding pages. That these implicit themes accompany all life events is natural to the human organism.

The presence of implicit themes makes inescapable
a multilevel structure of life. This conclusion has already been discussed. This structure exists for situation
jokes; it exists for all else that is called the ongoing

---

[1]There is strong evidence that a recognition of "joking" is
present in the joke-victim's brain, but this recognition will always be found to be an unconscious recognition, unavailable to
the awareness of the joke-victim. If it were otherwise, if the
joke-victim were aware of the "true" nature of the episode,
the joke would no longer be a joke and would become play between the joker and the joke-victim. It is implicit in the definition "practical joke" that whatever recognition the joke-victim has of the episode as a joke is unconscious recognition,
unavailable to him until the delivery of the punch line—that is,
when the purse is snatched away on the end of the string.

life process. As one is progressing through any particular portion of one's life, one is involved, on one level, in the explicit surface program. One is also involved, on many other levels, in the many conscious and unconscious programs that are implicit to the so-called "object" or "thing"—i.e., the "ongoing life process." It is as if we all lead many different lives at the same time, all on different levels of abstraction one from the other, and all interrelated comments on each other.

A situation (or "portion of one's life") becomes a situation joke when, through the operation of a punch line, those various levels are jumbled in such a manner that the rules for conceiving reality are changed. (This statement presents a partial view of the theory of the structure of humor that will be expanded through the rest of this book—particularly in the last two chapters.) Further, it is in the interrelationship of these many levels of abstraction involved in the "portion of life" which becomes a situation joke—it is in the interrelationship of these levels that the joke can be seen as a comment on itself. The portion of life which is the joke comments upon the joke which is the portion of life. As with the practical joke, both are the same, and each is different.

Much the same could be said about canned jokes. They are, in one way of speaking, the situation jokes of yesterday. Something funny occurs during the process of living. We have a situation joke. That situation joke is told twenty minutes later. Voilà! We have a canned joke. The canned joke is like a fish out of water. If, however, another look is taken, we can see that this fish carries his water with him. In sharing a canned joke, joker and audience are engaged, on one level, in participating in a portion of their "ongoing lives." The sharing of that joke constitutes the "life process" of the time being. And, from this standpoint is understood the emphasis in the canned joke definition placed on the word "obvious" ("little obvious relationship"). Discontinuous though the canned joke may seem, as regards the ongoing life process, the canned joke constitutes, in fact, a particular portion of the life process. (Furthermore, those higher-level aspects of a canned joke—the implicit themes that accompany, in the participants' brains, the canned joke—receive varying degrees of emphasis depending on the implicit themes that were active in the brain during the preceding moments. In other words, association is influenced by experience—both internal and external.) Again, is introduced the multilevel concept. The "ongoing life process" that is a canned joke is accompanied by many implicit themes on many different levels of abstraction. And, through the essential interrelatedness of the whole structure, the canned joke is, in one sense, itself and, in another sense, is comment on itself.

This realization of a joke as being both (1) a portion of the ongoing life process, and (2) a joke—this realization makes necessary a slight alteration in the usual way of thinking of the uniqueness and genuineness of the various particles of the world. In the next chapter it will be demonstrated that, through the agencies of the unconscious, an apparently artificial fol-de-rol such as a joke is inextricably more a part of the "genuine" stream of life than one might immediately suppose. The visions of the implicit that have been granted in the present chapter reinforce the demonstration. We find that, because of the presence of a multilevel structure—in humor, at least—the uniqueness of particles is mightily challenged. There certainly seems to be "more than meets the eye." It seems to be a fundamental characteristic of humor that, in the frame of humor, the pertinence of concepts such as "uniqueness" and "genuineness" is suspended.

Another area emphasized by the definitions of the three types of jokes needs elaboration. This area has to do with the personal involvements of the individual participants in the joke process. That there are individuals participating in humor should be obvious. Less obvious is the nature of the participation of each

individual.   (Considerable comment on this question
will appear in later chapters.)

The phrase "intrapsychic involvement" has been
used in these definitions.   What is meant is that internal, mental behavior—both conscious and unconscious—which is related to participation in humor.   We
cannot see what is going on inside a person's brain,
but certain guesses can be made about this internal involvement, on the basis of external observations.   With
canned jokes, the involvement is easily conjectured.
Both joker and audience are obviously aware that a
joke is being told.   The overt statement is made, "This
is a joke," "I want to tell you a funny story," or "Did
you hear this one?" etc.   All these introductory statements say that humor is being presented.   These statements also contain other, even more dynamic messages,
as will be seen later, but it can be agreed at this time
that they serve, at the least, to bring the participants
together into the humor episode.   And ostensibly, all
the assembled participants seem to be consciously aware
of the presence of humor.   You have only to walk into
a group of such joking persons to be made to realize
through the means of every possible communication
mode—verbal and nonverbal ("We are telling a joke,"
eye winks, facial expression, posture, voice tones, etc.)—
how much involved in the humor these participants are.

With those humor items termed practical jokes
the joker and the relatively uninvolved members of
the audience are overtly aware that a joke is in progress.   The victim (or victims) apparently does not
know.   Much of the artistry of the practical joke depends on the naïveté of the victim.   The victim in any
particular practical joke—like the purse-on-a-string
joke—has in his brain many implicit accompaniments
to his apparently unknowing participation in the joke.
Some of the accompaniments are what have been called
"merely implicit."   He may have the idea implicit to
finding an abandoned purse that he will soon become
wealthier than before this discovery.

Some accompaniments are unconsciously implicit. There is evidence that the victim has in his unconscious mind, inaccessible to awareness, the knowledge in one form or another that he is participating in a joke. Some subliminal signal has communicated the information, to be tucked away until the delivery of the "punch line" (in this case, the jerk of the purse by the string) confirms that the experience is a joke. Overtly, however, as far as can be distinguished from admittedly gross observation of the victim's behavior, he is unaware of the impending humor.

Finally, with situation jokes, it seems that none of the humor participants have knowledge of their impending involvement in a joke. If it were otherwise, we could call the episode by the name "canned joke" rather than by the name "situation joke." The participants seem innocent of their involvement until the punch line has been delivered and the laughter precipitated. Again, as above, we must indicate the reservation that an unconscious joke-knowledge is very possibly hidden somewhere inside the participants' neuronal pathways. But they do not appear to know it.

Through some of the peculiar things that have been written in this chapter, the reader is being asked to participate in some rather unfamiliar thinking. However, multilevelness, levels of abstraction, the implicit— all the phenomena discussed in this chapter are vital aspects of the human organism. Unfamiliar as they may seem, they are nevertheless as much a part of each individual "I" as a right thumbnail, or a left ear, or the warmest memory of one's childhood.

CHAPTER IV

The Unconscious

Any discussion on humor must refer emphatically to the unconscious. One of the great contributions of Freudian psychology has been the elaboration of the theory of the unconscious. Although this theory has many roots in pre-Freudian philosophy and psychology, Sigmund Freud and his disciples have done most in the formulation of the theory and in the development of various ramifications of it. They have sponsored most enthusiastically the recognition of the vital role of unconscious thought and motivation, not just in pathologic states, but in all human behavior. They are largely responsible for the almost automatic acceptance of the concept of the omnipresence of the unconscious mind. Previously, the unconscious was mystery, astrology, maybe even black magic—to be feared, or possessed of the Devil. Now the unconscious is the household cat, which goes its own way but is there, accepted by all.

The theory is that, with everything we do or think consciously, there are determinants or effects—concomitants—which do not register in awareness, but which are stored or are active elsewhere—in the unconscious mind. These unconscious thoughts or emotions, despite the fact that they are not apparent to us, are usually more powerful or influential than those of which we are aware. It is widely accepted that the unconscious—besides being a powerful controller and initiator of

57

mundane behavior—is also of vital importance in the
process of creation.   Numerous psychologic and psychoanalytic studies have traced down the individual unconscious origins of many manifestations of genius.   This
investigation has also been turned to humor with much
success.

It is curious to think of the original small Freudian
group, drawn together in Central Europe by the inspiration of one fevered genius—a man somewhat nervous,
persuasive, determined, and dedicated, occasionally
given to spells of intense fearfulness to the point of
hearing his own name called out by no one in the va-
cant streets, always inquiring and pushing further, himself his most valuable specimen, opening old scars in
the agonies of self analysis.   The thrill for the group
of them, all working together, discovering the unsus-
pected beneath the obvious, learning the power of understanding apparently unrelated events as parts of a whole,
charting areas of an unmapped continent—perhaps that
"outer world," Elysium, the paradise that the ancients
always knew was just beyond the turning point of the
voyage of the farthest ship out, just over the edge of
the farthest horizon.   The outer world that constitutes
the universe, that bounds the infinity our brains cannot
contain, that is ever retreating before our eyes and
finally, like the bluebird, is found back within ourselves.

Throughout history, mankind has dreamt of some
distant paradise, a land of curious and exotic glory.
The earliest map drawn from Hecataeus' travels and
the imagination of the times, shows the world bound in
its farthest extents by an unknown land, the outer bank
of the Oekenus ocean-stream, arching round in a complete embrace about the terrestial globe.   As exploration pushed the location of this unknown land always
further, people began to despair of its very existence.
Then came astronomy, and paradise jumped into the
starry wastes, to be called the universe.   But the universe won't stand still.   Its galaxies rush further from
us every microsecond.   And what is left, eventually,

are our dreams, our art, the household cat.   Perhaps
the explorer has always been looking into the wrong
end of the telescope to see what is itching his traveler's
heel. For the unconscious is a vast, almost unexplored
continent that bounds the world of each one of us, on
which our awareness lies floating. And, quite possibly,
in charting Oekenus and Elysium the ancients were trying to satisfy, on vellum, the curiosity aroused in themselves by the strange, compelling rumblings of each
one's private paradise and hell.

The Freudian group wrote extensively of their experiences. Freud, himself, could hardly have been more
prolific. In a rather large work, Wit and Its Relation
to the Unconscious, he originally presented a group of
ideas on how the unconscious operated in the case of
"wit" and the "comic." He described the need for wit
as "directed by an impulse to elude reason and substitute for the adult an infantile state of mind" and the
technique peculiar to wit as consisting of "a process
of safe-guarding the use of this pleasure-forming means
(i.e., wit) against the protest of reason which would
obviate the 'pleasure.'" A relationship (discussed
in a previous chapter) between humor and play was
emphasized in Freud's book. He maintained that the
pleasure obtained in humor results from a "removal of
inner inhibitions," that the energy for expression of
pleasure becomes available to the joker's audience in
overcoming repressions, suppressions, and inhibitions
associated with the material presented in the witticism—
i.e., that the energy for laughter "comes from libera-
tion and suspension of the inhibition cathexis." Wit was
characterized as making "use of a means of connection
(of ideas) which is rejected by, and carefully avoided
in serious thinking," and as containing "something familiar where one expects to find something new instead." Implied in his statements was a universal application of the unconscious.
There have been some cavils subsequently raised
against this work. One of these objections refers to

the title of the book—that it is about wit only, a very limited part of humor. That wit is but one pane in the window is true. However, the argument that since the Freudian studies were focused on wit (incidentally, wit is not the only form of humor considered in the book), then only wit could have unconscious content—this argument is nonsense. It would be the same to say that since Columbus sailed only one route in three bottoms on his discovery voyage to the lands of the fabled East, then only along those three tracks of water· actually traversed by the Nina, Pinta, and Santa María is the Earth curved into a round. With only Columbus' journey as evidence, the statement might be true, but not necessarily true. And so with humor, although the unconscious content of wit may be shown, this vision does not necessarily mean that the unconscious is active only in this small portion of humor.

In works subsequently published, the preliminary proposals of Freud have been expanded and applied in many other areas of the field of humor. In two recent books, Children's Humor, by Martha Wolfenstein, and Laughter and the Sense of Humor, by Edmund Bergler, one is able to discover the extent of this expansion. Psychoanalytic Explorations in Art, by Ernest Kris, who has spent much of his career considering the problems of the unconscious vis-à-vis Humor and the arts, gives an excellent picture of the value of the concept of the unconscious in the consideration of humor. The book Beyond Laughter, by Martin Grotjahn, must be mentioned in this context also. The unconscious is now found to be involved in all types of humor—in quite a vital way, as will be understood.

Consider several jokes and what might be one or two of the unconscious accompaniments to the humor. With this reservation in mind, that these here-printed "unconscious" themes will be recognized as artificial specimens—perhaps never an actual companion to a real, live joke-unfolding or perhaps only one of an unconscious troupe along with each particular joke.

First, a canned joke. A knight, sore-wounded after unsuccessful battle, is escaping through a dense and unknown forest, astride his rapidly failing trusty steed. After several hours, the horse can go no farther. The knight, knowing that he must go on, if only to gain shelter from a storm which warns of its close approach, dismounts and struggles on afoot.   Soon he falters. Just as he falls, exhausted, unable to take another step, a huge shaggy dog appears, motions to the knight to get aboard him, and goes off through the forest with the knight on his back. Then the storm breaks. Lightning, thunder, hail, rain. Drenching buckets of rain. At that point, there is seen the twinkling of a little light far off in the forest depths, and the dog, with the knight still astride, dashes toward this light. They find that the light is coming from the window of a poor, though well-constructed cabin. The dog raps on the door.   After a few moments, an old lady hesitantly opens the door and peers out into the storm. The knight tips his visor and requests lodging.   Just as the old lady is about to grant the wanderers entrance, a deep masculine voice comes from within, telling her to keep them out. She immediately protests, "Husband dear, you wouldn't keep a knight out on a dog like this."

The joke tells a story of a knight, a dog, and an elderly couple. But there is much more involved. Before examining one of the unconscious stories that might accompany or be stimulated by this joke, it is important to re-emphasize that such a story would, as stated, be but one of the many possible. It is an axiom that all symbols are multidetermined. The knight is a symbol for many things. The dog is a symbol for many things. And so on. Any story presented here is not the unconscious content, but merely may be an unconscious content. The purpose is not to analyze this joke, but rather to demonstrate the possibilities for analysis.

The unconscious tale could go as follows: A phallic symbol (knight) has lost his noble virility (horse). He comes upon anxiety-ridden times (storm), but is then supported by bestiality or an amoral attitude (shaggy dog). In this condition he comes to the embrace of his mother (cabin of the old lady) and expresses his need to enter. He is cut short in his application by the commanding voice of his father, refusing him such admission. (A triangular situation is thus constructed, and recapitulates the problems of the classic Oedipus problem.) But then the mother, utilizing an excellent word opportunity, reverses the usual "dog on a night like this" and protests that this knight-dog (incestuous penis) should be allowed the comforts of the night (sexual acceptance). This permission on the part of the mother is, of course, perfectly consistent in the unconscious terms presented. It is what one has unconsciously suspected all along—ever since it was set forth that the knight (penis) was impotent. It confirms that the incestuous phallus has suffered this impotence as a result of the temptations of a too-seductive mother and the subsequent guilt conflicts. (The story of King Oedipus also refers to such guilt castration when the king destroys his eyes—testes—upon learning the truth of his incest.)

As stated already, this is not the definitive unconscious analysis of this joke. There really is no one such analysis. Each symbol—the knight, for instance—is multidetermined. And this analysis is but one of many equally pertinent.

For the next example of unconscious content, we shall use a cartoon drawn by Phil Interlandi. In this picture are two businessmen sitting on a park bench. One is offering the other a cigarette from his pack while the other is shown as declining it. The legend under the picture contains the words of the offerer, "Whatcha trying to do, live forever?"

A story that might have been activated in the unconscious mind by this cartoon might involve the primary symbolization of the cigarette as a nurturing breast. It is refused. There must be something wrong with it (consciously—lung cancer?). That there is something wrong is confirmed by the legend (or punch line),

"Whatcha trying to do, live forever?" This question
and the refusal of the breast-cigarette refer back to
the unconscious concept that breasts might secrete a
poisonous substance, and are related to the unconscious
fear of the Spider-Mother.   The feelings of all of us
about our parents are complicated and multivalent. With
love of the child for the parent is also hatred-fear.
The inner image of the fear is the Spider-Mother, who
is puffed up with poison and malevolence.   The refusal
of the cigarette stimulates the image of the Spider-
Mother, strikes that chord in the unconscious mind.
The businessman is thus refusing a pull at his own
ambivalence.

In practical and situation jokes also, as well as in
canned jokes (exemplified by the shaggy dog story and
the cartoon), the unconscious themes are found. Take,
as an example of a good practical joke, the instance of
the by now legendary excavation of Fifth Avenue in New
York City.

A group of dedicated and inspired young men, under
the leadership of one of America's great practical
jokers, stole in upon the scene before dawn one day
during the early part of this century. Despite the fact
that the population of New York City then totaled perhaps two or three million persons less than at the time
of the writing of this book—despite that, Fifth Avenue
during the period marked by the commission of the
glorious outrage here related was already an extremely
important and busy street.   Before dawn, then, a section of the boulevard was effectively blocked off by
"Men Working" signs and the practical jokers went
about the business of confirming the honesty of the
signs.   They used picks and shovels and other destruc-
tive instruments, all with the net result that a considerable part of this busy artery had lost much of its
smooth paving surface within a fairly short period of
time.

No one stopped them, no one questioned their authority.   After they had torn up a large enough area,

they walked off, leaving holes, rubble, and blockade. Traffic movement was reputedly impossible for quite some time. The street section was devastated, but the ingenuity of confirmed and talented practical jokers was proved once again.

An unconscious companion of this episode might be formulated as having to do with the sexual frustrations of a group of young men, faced with the hard and un-yielding exterior (city-street pavement) of a desirable female (New York City). They are in love with a beau-tiful but cold creature. Their unhappy loneliness is the unhappy loneliness of every young person alone and isolated in a big city. They desire but cannot win their prize. Partly in fury and partly in love, they blockade this area of the beloved from the inroads of uncouth strangers and then proceed to rape her (dig holes with pick and shovel). Much satisfaction results and they walk off, satiated, leaving the ruined loved one.

There is no present way of knowing whether this theme actually ever was active in the unconscious minds of any of the jokers. But it <u>could</u> have been, and just as <u>it</u> could have been, so could have been one or sev-eral of many other themes. What we <u>can</u> be certain of is that this stunt did not involve <u>just</u> the digging up of a city street to the discomfiture of the motoring public.

Another practical joke which belongs to the ages is the one about the fake jewels. The episode involves the joker walking into a high-class jewelry store. He then inspects many fancy and expensive pieces, osten-sibly with an eye to purchase; but he finally decides not to buy anything. As he walks out, he drops a hand-ful of fake glass gems over the floor. (Another version of the joke involves the unobstrusive spilling of fake gems on the sidewalk outside a jewelry store.)

One of the unconscious themes which may be asso-ciated with this gag has to do with the symbolic identity between precious stones and feces. A man walks into a store and begins inspecting feces (gems). The gems-feces have both a great deal of value (gems, to the adult world, and feces, to the infant world) and no value at all (feces, to the adult world, and gems, to the infant world). This whole area of ambivalence is brought into focus—still unconsciously, of course—when the fake gems are defecated onto the floor like the feces they are and, when inspected, are revealed to be just as worthless (to the adult world) as the symbol mate—feces—has always been felt to be. In other words, the practical joke produces a re-enforcement of and referral to this unconscious identification of gems with feces.

An example of the action of the unconscious in situation humor can be found in the instances of an observer laughing at another person who has just fallen in the mud. A mud-fall is a fairly frequent occurrence, and it intermittently strikes one observer or another as amusing. A fall in the mud might be thought of as an involuntary return to pre-toilet training days, during which the infant is almost continuously "soiled." Toilet training, to a large degree, depends on the desire of the youngster to be like his elders, to maintain his position with them by acting "grown up," like a "little man" or a "little lady." To become soiled—by excreta or mud—means that one is childish, unable to control bodily functions, at the mercy of "crude" bodily forces and unable to direct his destiny by cerebral powers. The fall in the mud then stimulates, among other things, an unconscious perception of the faller as like a child again.

Another instance of situation humor can be discussed—to tie up the bundle. Considerable amusement (and some sadness) was generated among a group of psychiatrists over a real-life tableau that was described to them. The tableau had three players, all men. They had been standing together one evening in a row outside a small building, each intensely concentrated on his particular activity.   One man had been vomiting, one man had been publicly urinating, and the third had been gazing at the moon, head thrown back, arms outstretched, a picture of unswerving and ecstatic worship.

The men were on the grounds of a hospital exclusively concerned with the care of persons who suffered with emotional and mental illnesses. They were patients of the hospital. There was no contrivance in their having come together at that particular time for their individual activities. They just happened to be there together.   And it just happened that they were observed by someone who was in such a mood that the tableau seemed humorous.   And it just happened further that the story was passed on to a group of persons who were in such a mood that the tableau represented a kind of joke to them also.

But what might be an unconscious theme unfurled under the stimulation of this tableau?   The actors in this play were psychotic patients, presumably suffering with schizophrenia. The audience consisted of psychiatrists concerned with the admittedly difficult problems of treating that painful illness. The vomiting man could have symbolized the nausea a psychiatrist sometimes feels when contemplating the difficulties of helping an individual stricken with schizophrenia. The urinating man could have symbolically expressed for one or another of the audience the irritation that may result from frustrations of the therapist's attempts to help the psychotic patient in his struggles against his illness.

And what of the moon-gazer?   He, in a way, was sort of a punch line to the whole episode.   His rapt contemplation was an element crucial for the production of humor.   It could have been that his part in the tableau embodied the awe and wonder that all people dealing with emotional and mental illnesses come to develop concerning the complexities and brilliances of the human mind.   The object of worship—the "man in the moon," long associated in some strange way with insanity, "lunacy"—becomes representative of the inscrutable and

glorious madness of all men's minds. And the worship-
ping patient becomes his counterpart, the psychiatrist.

This exposition on the unconscious aspects of humor
has been presented not to demonstrate my familiarity
with Freud's lectures, but rather to emphasize a particular, vital point about humor. This is a point which
is often missed or forgotten. In studies and in talk,
humor is frequently treated as a completely artificial
phenomenon—something which happens and, in that sense
only, is related to the larger lives of the participants,
but which is detached otherwise from life and, by its
nature, has nothing to do with the ongoing process of
living. Now, for the type of humor which I have called
situation humor, such a treatment is obviously absurd.
But, also, this description of the other two types of
humor is equally blind. By these bridges of the unconscious the stream between humor and life is crossed
and recrossed, and there is found to be ample traffic
from shore to shore. Humor can only be drawn out
from life, condensed away from living by specialized,
philosophic techniques—techniques which, as in the case
of the preparation of tissues for microscopic examination, distort and twist and render humor examined as
different from humor lived.
When biologic tissue was first prepared for microscopic study, it was not known to what great extent
distortion was produced. It was assumed that the living cell was quite similar to the parboiled, desiccated
result spread on the glass slide. But, as tissue science has advanced, the extent of alteration has received
increasing consideration and a whole subspecialty has
grown up concerning the allowances required for known
distortions. In the preceding material on the unconscious aspects of humor, it has been necessary to con-
dense and desiccate. It has been practical to present
only part of the complex unconscious process stimulated
by humor. In what follows, also, the techniques necessary to presenting a discussion of a phenomenon like
humor will involve distortion. If, however, one is aware

of the loci and directions of distortion, one can proceed, making internal corrections and getting a fairly
reasonable picture of the living phenomena under discussion.   For humor is certainly living; it is broad-
cast and many-headed.   The unconscious mind springs
out from its position in the center of the individual
life and, in many ways and places, crosses to the vi-
brant shore of humor.

These unconscious bridges become connectors between humor and everything else in the human world.
Because of the operation of the unconscious mind, it
is impossible to affirm humor to be a thing alone and
separate.   Because of the unconscious, when a person
hears or tells a joke, the incident is not an independent frivolity—unrelated to the deeper currents and meanings of that person's life.   Through the agency of the
unconscious, that joke—heard or told—is undeniably
linked with all in the person's life that has gone on
before or will follow thereafter.

CHAPTER V

Levels of Living

It may be exceedingly difficult for most of us to conceive of smiling, laughter, and humor as being anything but pleasureful and desirable. These phenomena brighten many of our living hours, produce much entertainment, even relieve suffering and sometimes despair. One should never be thought of as unimaginative because of not having at some time or another conceived the idea that humor might be associated with distress for certain persons. In the ordinary flow of life, a person—unless he happens to have come into contact with one of those unfortunate individuals to whom humor means less than pleasure—would not be expected to consider that humor might be intentionally and steadfastly avoided by certain individuals who suffer torment as a result of contact with it. But, although this possibility is not a threat to most of us, it is, for a small group, grimly present.

There are, in fact however, some persons—admittedly few in number—, to whom humor represents not a pleasure and a boon, but a curse. Instead of seeking out the opportunities to laugh and joke, these persons avoid humor assiduously. Because of the nature of their reaction to humor, they must control their lives in such ways as to diminish contacts with it to the irreducible minimum.

Some of the rest of us may be somewhat dour or
tend to avoid humor because of rigid aesthetic or religious attitudes. These latter persons are not forced
to avoid humor because of unpleasantness consequent to
it; they choose to do so because of some personal pen-
chant. Their reasoning has led them to this point, and
they have enlisted their self-will on the side of preference. This is not the case for the persons who serve
as the focus of this chapter. Their preference may be
wholeheartedly for humor, but, whereas their desire
for it may be strong, they are forced by their own
selves to eschew the humorous. They find that the
consequences of their indulgence in the enjoyment of
humor are irresistible. Their only answer is to avoid
involvement.

In contradistinction to the dourness and preferential
moroseness of "professional" tragedians, the victims of
the pathology to be described here may be basically
quite merry. But they have been placed, by their disorder, in the dilemma of being unable to give full lib-
erty to their tendencies towards merriment. They are
forced to resort to techniques of avoidance and non-
participation in order to minimize their pathologic reactions. They must draw a somber cloak about and risk
the disappointment of those who attempt to amuse them,
as the better of two evils.

Cataplexy, the condition that requires such sacri-
fice on the part of its victims, is a very odd and fortu-
nately rare malady involving intermittent loss of skeletal muscle power. This weakness comes over a patient
victimized by the illness upon stimulation within him
of some emotion—most frequently amusement. The attack is almost instantaneous and may last several minutes, during which the patient may have collapsed help-
lessly to the ground, or may have just barely been able
to cling to some supporting object. Consciousness is
not usually disturbed; the victim is hindered in his
speech, but by weakness rather than by insensibility.
The recovery from the collapse may be gradual or

rapid, lasting several minutes or only a few seconds. Another spell may appear within minutes after recovery from the first. The illness does not seem to be hereditary. It may appear in an otherwise perfectly healthy individual. It may arise in the patient's life without precedent, without warning.

Cataplexy is frequently accompanied in its appearance by the conditions called narcolepsy and sleep paralysis, or it may appear alone. Briefly—because we are not directly concerned with them here—narcolepsy is an illness involving an uncommonly frequent and irresistible tendency to fall asleep at random intervals. Sleep paralysis is manifested by intermittent awakenings from sleep to a condition of muscular paralysis; the victim awakens from his slumber to find himself unable to use the power of his skeletal muscles.

A cataplexy attack typically occurs with the patient in the position of experiencing an unexpected or inevitable emotion. If the patient is able to avoid becoming emotionally involved, that is, if he is aware of the potentials of his situation and if he is capable of using his knowledge to his advantage, the attack may be aborted. But if unexpected or inevitable emotion appears within the victim, he then begins to experience a rapidly spreading muscular weakness which finally results in varying degrees of collapse. The skeletal muscles—the voluntary muscles, most prominently those of the arms, legs, shoulders, neck, and back—become progressively less responsive to the victim's attempts to tighten them. Although vital functions are mercifully not involved in this reaction, and fatalities are rare, the experience is said to be distinctly unpleasant; those who suffer from the disease sometimes go to great lengths to avoid stimulation of their symptom.

After an indefinite period of helpless paralysis, the victim, usually by now the center of much distressed attention on the part of those about him, begins to be able to call forth some response to his desires in first one muscle, and then another. Strength returns either slowly, during a period of several minutes, gradually spreading over the whole mass of involved musculature, or recovery may be quite rapid, within seconds, and the victim may literally be able to jump to his feet from his state of humiliating weakness.

Usually the persons suffering with this trouble are free of disorder between each specific attack of weakness. In the interim they find no immediate reason to feel that they are the victims of a strange malady. The cataplexy victim generally finds himself or herself able to carry on a life that would be considered quite normal—except that he must effect some changes in his emotional existence to allay or abort the potential attack of paralysis that is always around the corner of the next laugh, etc.

Amusement appears to be the most active emotion. It is more frequently spoken of as the precipitating mood in cataplexy production than other emotion. Besides amusement, other emotions which can be followed by this collapse are anger, surprise, fear, sudden fright or alarm, triumphant satisfaction, embarrassment. Many of the "emotions" to which persons refer are not really what we know as simple emotions, but are very complicated composites of the so-called simple emotions. These composites are often so complicated as to be difficult to describe. A more satisfactory exposition of this matter can be presented by discussing some actual cataplectic experiences.

Let us first deal with amusement situations. Some sufferers have cataplexy appearing only after the actual onset of laughter; others experience the weakness as direct response to humor, before the appearance of laughter. The latter is such a strong tendency in some that they are never able to laugh. They become paralyzed, and physically unable to laugh, in every circumstance that might potentially allow for laughter. (This observation would seem to confirm that, for some at least, it is truly the humor presented and not necessarily the muscular behavior involved in smiling or laughing that is the precipitating agent of the weakness seizures—that the cataplexy activation takes place some time before the laugh muscle effectors are fired off in the brain.

The amusement that stimulates cataplexy can be occasioned by any one of the three varieties of humor I have designated in this book. Canned humor—such as jokes told by one person to another, funny movies, newspaper comics, vaudeville and burlesque, or humor as presented in the theater—all have been reported as stimulators of the cataplectic weakness. Some victims state that whenever anyone tells them a joke, they are overcome by sudden weakness. If they were so indiscreet as to tell a joke themselves, the subsequent weakness would be that much more widespread and profound. Others have reported that they can safely tell jokes themselves if they do not smile or chuckle, but that as soon as the person to whom the joke is addressed begins to laugh, the teller is seized by cataplexy. Still others relate that they are able to tell jokes, and enjoy the amusement of those to whom the joke is directed, but become weakened if they are told a joke by someone else. A few persons indicate that if they even think of a joke, weakness results forthwith. Several patients have reported to their doctors that merely overhearing a joke told by a stranger to other strangers—all of whom may be completely unaware of the attention or presence of the cataplexy victim—stimulates paralysis.

Teasing, tickling, jesting, and other forms of situation humor can produce paralysis attacks. Some patients experience weakness as soon as they extend a finger to tickle another person; others do not become weak until their finger actually makes contact with the person to be tickled. The pleasures of playing with their children are severely curtailed for some victims. If the play turns up situation humor, as play frequently does, cataplexy results. Many victims of the malady have found it necessary to give up the enjoyment of bridge, or chess, or checkers, or other similar games because of the likelihood of paralysis following merriment

generated during such friendly competitions. Friendly
arguments or conscious bragging about oneself—when
accompanied by humor—have stimulated weakness in
susceptible persons. Some persons have reported paralysis attacks consequent on the attempt to tease by
mocking the manner of another person—for example, by
assuming an exaggeratedly serious mien to satirize an
unappreciated desire on the part of another to enter
upon sober concerns, thus being serious for humerous
purposes. These various possibilities all extend over
to the other half of the picture, in which the cataplexy
patient is the object of the teasing, tickling, and the
like, and is then seized by weakness.

Similarly, the patient finds the same difficulty in
being the perpetrator or the victim of a practical joke.
Many patients have had to give up indulgence in practical jokes altogether. A mother suffering with this condition found that she was no longer able to indulge in
the innocent fun of a practical joke on her daughter's
boy friend, in which she pretended to be the daughter
when he called on the telephone. This joking deception
would cause her to experience cataplectic weakness.
Various patients have reported experiencing cataplexy
attacks when being made the victim of a practical joke.
One can imagine the importance to these unfortunate
people of not attempting to pick up a purse lying unattended on the sidewalk on April Fools' Day, lest the
patient find himself dropped full to the pavement by the
flick of an unseen thread and his own sudden weakness.

Humor, laughter, and smiling are not the only stimulators of spells of cataplexy. There are many other
culprits. Typical situations involving the appearance of
other stimulating emotions include anger at a child's
disobedience, meeting a friend unexpectedly in the street,
hearing a telephone bell ring, being suddenly aware of
the presence of a poisonous snake, finding an examination question that is beyond the patient's knowledge,
spilling food at the dinner table, being unexpectedly
shouted at. All of these have been followed by sudden
collapse on the part of susceptible individuals.

Further, more complicated experiences are reported as equally pernicious. A patient stated that he may walk up the steps to the front door of a friend's house and be prepared to ring the doorbell. He extends his finger toward the doorbell button and, at the moment of contact, experiences a cataplectic attack. Or a patient may see a person on the street whom he would prefer to ignore by feigned failure to recognize. But the other person has already become aware of the patient's presence and has indicated that he knows the patient has seen him. To avoid the appearance of rudeness, the patient is forced to the decision that he must make some gesture toward the other. As he lifts his hand for a friendly wave or as he tenses his leg muscles for a step in the direction of the other person, weakness suddenly comes over him. A victim of the illness spoke of the experience of telling someone quite important in his life—mother, wife, father—of an important decision. At the point, following the preliminaries, when the decision is to be placed before the other person, the patient experiences cataplexy.

Hunting seems to be loaded with cataplexy-precipitating experiences. A patient reported being seized by weakness simply upon being surprised by the sudden noise of a shotgun discharge. In an extensive study which has contributed valuable information about this disease, Dr. Howard Fabing quotes a patient as stating that he would suffer cataplectic weakness when he raised his gun to his shoulder to shoot the game. This patient, and others, also found the symptom precipitated by the sudden, jump-up appearance of a rabbit or the call of a quail. Another patient was able to pass all these hazards, fire his gun, and hit the bird, only to slump in a cataplectic reaction as the bird fell to the ground. This situation has a parallel in fishing when the patient is struck by weakness upon hooking his fish, and is prevented from being able to land his prize. Or paralysis may appear upon swatting a fly, killing a moth, or squashing a bug.

Winning at cards, checkers, chess, poker, etc., is difficult. Patients have reported that just as the poker pot is reached for, so that it may be drawn in, weakness sets in. Dr. Harry Cave, in one of the earlier papers written in the United States about cataplexy, describes a patient whose weakness appeared at exciting moments in card games—such as the moment when he was able to play the highest trump and take the trick. The taking of a checker or chess piece may cause a sudden cataplectic weakness. Outdoor sports are also involved. A patient would catch a fly ball in a game of baseball, only to collapse with paralysis. A patient reported attempting to tag a man out as he slid onto base and being prevented by the appearance of his symptom. He might hit a homer and be prevented from starting out around the bases by sudden weakness.

Relationships with children also have strong potential for symptom precipitation. Besides teasing and playing games with children, which may contain humor, scolding or spanking children may produce an attack. One patient invariably found himself incapacitated by his cataplexy whenever he would attempt to spank his child. The child would be in position across the knees, the father's hand would be raised ready to spank. And just as the spank was to be delivered, the father would suddenly become weak. The reverse of such experiences may be found in another patient's report that memories of her own childhood and specific episodes involving herself and her parents stimulated sudden weakness—each time she recalled the "meanness" of her parents, she would become liable to paralysis. A patient reported the embarrassing experience of finding it necessary to scold a misbehaving student, only to be prevented from carrying out this responsibility because an attack of her weakness had caused her to slump to the floor.

Husband-wife relationships can become involved in the illness. A wife kissed her husband and slumped into his arms, not with passion but from an attack of cataplexy. Patients have complained of the loss of the ultimate pleasures of sexual intercourse, in that they may engage with enjoyment in all the foreplay of sexual relations, but are robbed of orgasm by the appearance of their symptom just before the moment of climax.

There are many, many other examples which could be presented—either of episodes involving the combination of cataplexy and simple emotion or of episodes involving the appearance of the paralysis during the process of an extremely involved and complex experience. If one wished to construct some generalizations about cataplexy, it would be rather difficult to generalize about the emotional mechanisms responsible for triggering the cataplectic attacks. Some of the triggering experiences are so simple, and some are so complex. Generalization, under these circumstances, presents a real challenge.

Throughout all these experiences, it is insisted repeatedly that the mind is clear, that at no time, even at the most profound depth of the attack, is there any clouding of consciousness. The patient is aware of everything about him; he understands questions (but is physically unable to answer) and conversation; he is able to observe his own state and the distress of those around him. The paralysis itself is not such a constant thing as this clearness of the mind. The patient may find himself so paralyzed as to be limp like a rag doll, or he may find that the attack has produced some degree of weakness rather less than complete collapse. Simple weakness of the knees, legs, or neck may be found; sometimes an isolated weakness may appear in the limbs involved in the activity which might be said to have stimulated the attack, such as an isolated weakness of the right arm and hand as one is about to take the bridge trick by putting out an ace. The fact that few people suffer any serious injury as a result of their spells of paralysis is a fair measure of the variable nature of the intensity of the weakness. Seeing a poisonous snake in the water under the foot-bridge one is crossing and developing a cataplectic attack would likely produce very unpleasant results if one were suddenly

paralyzed to the point of being unable to prevent oneself
from pitching off the bridge and joining the snake below.
Despite the seemingly ample opportunity for injury with
this illness, little serious injury does occur. It has
been phrased by one patient, "Being in real danger
seems to snap me out of going on and having one of
my spells."

One wonders, on the basis of this information, what
influences might modify the cataplectic spell—either to
intensify or to ameliorate it. We have, for instance,
the testimony that an attack will be less paralyzing if
the more profound weakness would result in serious
harm to the patient. A rule of self-preservation seems
to be involved. Not only is the reaction produced as
a result of the patient's perception of the situation
in which he finds himself, but also it may be modified
in its intensity by some aspect of that same perception.

There are other influences or circumstances that
are responsible for alterations of the cataplexy pattern.
Some women report that their cataplectic spells tend
to be more frequent and more severe preceding and
during menstruation. Pregnancy has increased the sev-
erity of the disorder. Decreased frequency of sexual
intercourse has resulted in a temporary decrease in the
frequency of the spells; on the other hand, the intensity
of weakness seems increased by abstinence. The in-
gestion of alcohol may result in decrease of both frequency and intensity; but, the patient pays double fold
the next day, when he is subject to the hangover penalty
of more attacks than on a normal day. Some victims
have their attacks only in the privacy of their homes,
others at work or in the streets. For others, the significance of context is more obscure. Few attacks of
paralysis ever take place, strangely enough, in the presence of a physician. Patients have reported that they
can count on a marked decrease of their symptomatology on those days when they may be visiting the doctor.

The influences described above are more or less unplanned. They are ordinary matters not especially related to the fact of a person suffering with cataplexy. There are also what might be called contrived influences that can affect the cataplexy pattern—influences that are particularly devised to cause some change in the pattern. One type of such influence may be exerted by the medication prescribed for relief of the illness. Certain preparations—notably potassium salts, phenacemide, amphetamine, ephedrine, dibenzylmethylamine, pituitary extract—have been found to be helpful, in some cases causing a disappearance of the symptoms. As another type of influence, patients report various techniques they have discovered for protecting themselves from the intensity of their illness. In studying the nature of these techniques, we find, surprisingly enough, a solution to the problem of generalizing about the emotional mechanisms responsible for triggering the paralysis attacks.

The information reported by patients who have used self-protection techniques has led to the conclusion that they engage in an operation that must result in a falsification of the validity of their involvement in emotional experience. As indicated in the preliminary remarks on this illness, distance—in an emotional sense, emotional distance or noninvolvement—will abort the cataplexy attack. Distance could be obtained by physically isolating oneself, away from all interpersonal and emotion-laden relationships. One could, for instance, become a hermit. But this is obviously very difficult to manage and, besides, there are emotional experiences which do not directly involve face-to-face interpersonal relationships. The hermit could walk over a bridge and see a snake in the water below. So, that sort of distance is difficult, lonely, and not infallible.

To falsify by internal adjustment the validity of one's emotional involvement also obtains distance (emotional distance). Falsification-distance can be achieved in almost any situation, providing one is not too much taken by surprise or the emotion is not overwhelmingly

compelling. It exacts a terrible price, but this is a
price many people would be willing to pay in face of
the alternative of repeated attacks of uncontrolled weakness. On one hand is the price one pays of relinquish-
ing the freshness of a spontaneous and genuine feeling;
on the other are the many embarrassing falls, the humiliating and difficult-to-explain halts in the process of
the ongoing behavior, the questioning glances and whis-
pered comments, etc. Many patients apparently prefer
to attempt to change the internal balance of their emotional lives rather than continue with the full intensity
of their illness.

The concept of falsification of one's emotional life
may be somewhat obscure. Some further discussion of
this concept might be in order. Cataplexy victims describe what they do to themselves to abort attacks in
such terms as the following. A patient reported to Dr.
John B. Dynes that, in the face of a tendency to development of sudden weakness with laughter, joviality, or
other merriment, he forced onto himself a "glum and
pessimistic attitude." And, by this general tendency to
see the worst side of everything, he was protected from
the encroachments of most amusement and the subsequent paralysis attack. If the humor-cataplexy linkage
is more specific and the weakness appears only with
the stimulus of a deep belly-laugh, this reaction has
sometimes been prevented by the hasty substitution of
a high, twittering laugh. The substitute laugh may serve
as a manifestation of genuine amusement yet also gov-
ern, by its artificiality, the intensity of the gleefulness.
Dr. Fabing's patient laughed only with a "hollow laugh."
Others report a "laconic laugh." In an another article
on cataplexy written by Dr. Dynes it was reported that
a patient allowed himself a "quiet chuckle" as an expression of humor. Patients quoted by Dr. Cave spoke
of forcing themselves out of their humorous mood by
"becoming serious" in their conversation and of obtaining partial control over their symptoms by "putting
their minds to it," or by doing what is vaguely known

as "exerting conscious effort." Still others report in-
terrupting the ongoing, spontaneous, or genuine stream
of life—which would eventually be marked by a cataplexy attack—by pinching themselves as those situations
develop which they have learned usually result in paralysis.   Or they may assume a certain posture which is
helpful in establishing discontinuity, or may tense some
particular muscle like the tongue or the biceps.   (All
of which is somewhat reminiscent of the habit of counting the dance steps to prevent oneself from falling in
love with one's dancing partner.)

With examination and analysis of these various control operations—hollow laugh, pinch, becoming serious,
etc.—a common denominator becomes more obvious.
These various techniques, in achieving the objective of
falsification, interrupt the ongoing process of life.   In
this interruption, a person is brought to a position of
increased self-awareness, or increased self-consciousness.   He is reminded, by the necessity of producing
a laugh that is a metaphor of real laugh, of his location in the flow of things.   He may become aware that
a laugh is appropriate under the particular circumstances.   Instead of naturally laughing as the flow of
things dictates, he pegs himself in the flow and manu-
factures a laugh, realizing that a laugh is appropriate—
and also that a manufactured laugh will be less likely
to stimulate cataplexy than a natural laugh.   The patient,
it is true, takes part in the spontaneous chain of events
that would ordinarily be assumed to make up his life;
but he is also ever on the watch, observing himself for
possibly dangerous involvements.

We all—patients and not—exist not only on the so-
called primary level of existence, but also on other,
meta-, or observational levels.   We all are both in
being and aware of being—both in regard to internal
events and with respect to our external relationships.
But whereas most of us tend to accentuate in our awareness the ongoing flow, or primary level of existence,
the cataplexy patient finds it advisable to emphasize the
observational or meta-level aspect.   He might be said
to have always a specific opinion about the moment.

Perhaps the term "falsification" is not the most
lucid that might be used in this context. The preferred
word (which does not seem to exist in our English vocabulary) would properly have several of the connotations of <u>falsification</u>, in that the operation described is
contrived, nonprimary, purposeful—as much advertising
for food products represents a falsification of the natural, biologic appetite of living creatures. In this context, we are reminded of the meaning of the word "<u>fac-
titious</u>." But the word that we desire would also have
connotations of metaphorizing—in that the behavior involved in the falsification operation becomes, by reason
of that operation, metaphoric for that natural behavior
which is rendered <u>hors de combat</u> by the metaphoric
behavior. The nonexistent word also would represent
the concept of <u>replacement</u>—that which indicates how
completely one's participation in the ongoing, unself-
conscious, natural behavior of life is replaced, altered,
invalidated, or interrupted by the introduction of a self-
conscious and purposeful attitude. It is a biologic impossibility for a creature to exist on one level of involvement and to be aware at the same time of that
one-level existence. By definition, the fact of awareness introduces secondary, observational or meta-levels,
and the primary-level existence is replaced by a far
more complex structure. Once having made the awareness jump (eaten the fruit of the Tree of Knowledge),
we acquire meta-levels galore. There can be awareness of awareness of awareness, and so on. There
are, in addition, possibilities of branching in this hierarchy—for example, one becomes aware that such an
awareness hierarchy exists. With each additional jump,
we conquer a new observation post from which to look
down upon ourselves.

The problem of generalizing about the emotional
mechanisms which trigger cataplexy is then somewhat
clarified by being able, by virtue of the material just
discussed, to say that cataplexy is stimulated in "spontaneous" or "genuine" or "natural" situations. The
cataplectic attack is dependent on a minimum of self-

awareness or self-consciousness and a maximum of being immersed in the flow of life. It has been demonstrated, by experimentation, that it is quite difficult to induce intentionally such an attack. You cannot just say, "I'm going to have an attack," and will yourself into one. It is rather like the problem of constipation, in which the intention of having a bowel movement becomes one of the important factors rendering that intention less likely of fulfillment. The paralysis will not come when it is sought for. So, instead of saying that cataplexy is the exclusive province of one emotion or another—amusement, anger, or the like—we find that the generalization concerns the nature of the emotion, and learn that paralysis will occur as a "spontaneous" event, stimulated by "spontaneous" emotions.

In this generalization is found an interesting similarity between cataplexy and the problem of impotence. Obviously, the cataplectic attack and the sexual orgasm are both members of the broad category of physiologic phenomena known as "release phenomena." Further, the problem of spontaneity versus contrivance seems quite pertinent to impotence, as well as to cataplexy. What the victim of impotence finds, to his discomfort, is that the more he tries to overcome his symptom, the worse his condition becomes. The more he attempts to force an orgasm, the farther from his goal he finds himself. An orgasm, like a cataplectic attack, cannot be willed. Indeed, as one becomes more aware of the possibility of orgasm and as one focuses more intently on that possibility, then one finds that possibility is less available.

It could be postulated that some degree of self-induced hypnotic trance is necessary during orgasm. In experimental hypnosis, self-awareness or self-contemplation can be disruptive to the trance state and requires covering by special instructions. The actual decrease of awareness of a person in sexual ecstasy is proverbial—the wallet of the prostitute's customer disappears as he experiences his orgasm. It is a fundamental truth that spontaneity cannot be forced.

"Having a specific opinion about the moment" is apparently antagonistic to having an orgasm—in the context of impotence.

The general importance of all this information applies to the area of involuntary behavior. The conclusion is that insofar as a cataplectic attack represents a involuntary act of a human organism—that is, the contributing involuntary physiology—to that extent can the involuntary be said to be made voluntary. Certainly, one can voluntarily relax and contract the skeletal muscles that might become involved in cataplexy. But a cataplectic attack is not that sort of thing. In an attack, the patient does not voluntarily relax his muscles. He cannot will a cataplectic attack, nor can he prevent one by directly attacking the oncoming muscle weakness. The cataplectic seizure must be classified, in general, as an involuntary phenomenon. And yet, some influence over this involuntary phenomenon can be created by "coming round Robin Hood's barn," so to speak, in the indirect approach discussed above. Orgasm, which is similarly considered to be an involuntary phenomenon, actually under the control of the autonomic nervous system, a nervous system operative on a far deeper physiologic level than that nervous system which allows us to move our hand when we want to do so—orgasm also is subject to this indirect but voluntary influence. It can be hastened by certain thoughts and it can be deferred by others. Varying degrees of impotence can be found associated with volition. The underlying physiology remains involuntary, but it can be influenced significantly by voluntary use of this technique of emphasizing an observational or meta-level involvement.

In hypnosis, we find this influence over the so-called involuntary phenomena demonstrated even more dramatically. One episode comes to mind immediately. A boy fell and badly injured his face, causing fractures of his nose, upper jaw, and upper front teeth. An oral surgeon was called for emergency treatment, but was handicapped in his work by profuse bleeding from the injured area and by the boy's reactions to the terrible

pain he suffered.   Hypnosis was suggested as of some
benefit in controlling these factors.   One of the oral
surgeon's colleagues helped the boy into a hypnotic
trance and suggested that the boy be free of his pain.
The suggestion was successful.   The hypnotist then suggested that the boy "turn off the faucet" that was pouring all that blood from the injured area.   The effect of
this suggestion was that the hemorrhage was immediately slowed to gentle ooze!   And the oral surgeon was
able to perform his treatment at will.   I, myself, suffered one season with a bad case of poison-oak reaction.   Hopefully, I persuaded a colleague to try hypnotic
suggestion as a therapy for my condition.   The treatment was given, and one or two hours later my itching
became more benign than it had been for days.   More
important, the reaction itself began to involute within
twenty-four hours.

Warts have been caused to disappear through the
use of hypnosis.   Operations have been performed with
profound physiologic controls established as results of
hypnosis techniques.   The voluntary influences over pain
perception, temperature perception, muscle strength,
and other involuntary phenomena that can be achieved
in hypnotic trance are familiar to all.   One particularly
striking example is that of the appearance, under hypnotic trance, of the Babinski toe reflex.   This primitive
nerve-muscle reflex is one which is usually active during the early months of a human being's life, but which
usually vanishes at the age of one to one and a half
years.   It becomes active again in later years only if
profound neurologic disease exists.   Except—if an individual in hypnotic trance is suggested back into the first
months of life, the Babinski reflex may become active
once more.

Hypnosis is not strictly comparable with the "falsification" operations used by cataplexy patients to influence their symptomatology.   There is, however, much
evidence to suggest that the underlying phenomenon in
both hypnosis and falsification are comparable.   Like
the falsification, hypnosis seems to utilize a manipulation of the levels of awareness and involvement.

The conclusion that inner physiology can be so influenced by mental behavior seems to be inescapable. The emphasis of the cataplexy patient on a multilevel participation in life results in his increased ability to control his symptoms. Laughing a "hollow laugh" has less chance of precipitating cataplectic weakness than laughing spontaneously, and so on.

It could be argued, of course, that any volitional act will have its physiologic influences. For instance, running up stairs will increase the heart rate, increase the systolic blood pressure, etc. Looking at a bright light will result in a constriction of the pupil of the eye. Yet this viewpoint is a rather unusual one in Western civilization, where a strong line is drawn between the so-called voluntary and involuntary functions of the human organism. The orientation, emphasized in this study of cataplexy, that basic physiology is actually open to influence by conscious intent is somewhat novel to Western thought.

With such considerations as these in mind, we are reminded of strange phenomena from other cultures. We are reminded of the death magic of various primitive civilizations—for instance, that of the Trobriand people, as described by Bronislaw Malinowski. This magic involves the casting of a spell against the health of a person by a sorcerer. The ultimate act in this magic is the virulent rite of the "pointing bone." If not counteracted by other, more powerful magic, this rite may result in the death of the victim. Apparently, being the object of this sort of magic involves a profound psychologic effect that eventually influences body physiology to the extent that death results.

We are reminded also of the conscious influencing of body metabolism which will enable a fakir to fast for what seems to be an incredible length of time. Or we may be reminded of the fakir's volitional influence over pain mechanisms which makes it possible to accomplish some of the rituals that so often seem to involve what should be ghastly agony to the performer. (I suppose the reductio ad absurdum of this sort of

thing would be a supposed purposive physiologic disinte-
gration that occurs when the fakir climbs to the top of
the Indian rope and disappears.)

In a larger sense, these considerations on physiology, purpose, and influence have certain philosophic
pertinence. The thinkers of various Western cultures
have been concerned for centuries with the question of
man or God, of divine or human spirituality or mind
versus nature or body. Heaven is set up against earth.
The soul is contrasted with the flesh. In this context,
nature works against morality or human intelligence.
Nature is described as a power, something for humanity
to conquer or be conquered by. Man conquers space,
the wastelands, and the oceans, harnesses the tides,
stems the floods, survives the storms, escapes the
whirlwinds, reaps the winds, and so on. The assumption is implied that a state of mutual opposition exists
between humanity and nature. Nature is thought of as
hostile to man, and insofar as man is natural, or a
part of nature, he is weak and doomed to failure in his
attempts to attain the divine. Biblical prophets and
disciples experience failure in their search for union
with God because of their "fleshly weaknesses," their
bonds with nature. "The spirit is willing, but the flesh
is weak." Further, nature is irrational, without purpose or order or goals; it is wild ("living in a state
of nature") and savage. It is desolate, without bounds,
endless, and without beginning. Man fights throughout
his life against nature, always defining, organizing, tim-
ing, structuring, conquering, only to disappear in the
end with a final defeat into its indefinable and unmeas-
urable purposelessness.

These remarks are prefaced with the statement
that such matters are the concern of philosophers in-
digenous to various Western cultures. There are certain of the Eastern philosophies which eschew such a
dichotomous relationship between man-in-the-image-of-
God and nature. Zen Buddhism is one such. Zen is
a religion-philosophy involving a series of experiences
for the initiate that ultimately leads him to an inner

enlightenment. That enlightenment is characterized as a psychologic (or psychophysiologic) event wherein the individual is suddenly aware of a structure of reality that is called "ultimate" and is spoken of as a moment of "timelessness," a place without intellectual behavior or consciousness, beyond dichotomies or classifications, where pure subjectivity becomes pure objectivity, where I am I and you are you and yet I am you and you are I. In this place, man is in nature and nature is in him. The sea and the land is in man, man is in the sea and the land; man sees the sea and the land, the sea and the land see man. Without loss of any bit of the component parts, man and nature are found in identity.

This way of experiencing life is unfamiliar to Western minds. It is, by its nature, inconceivable. For by the fact of attempting the conception of this event of enlightenment is made impossible the experiencing of the enlightenment itself. The enlightenment must, it is said, come in the process of living. It is an "aha" sort of experience, rather than a "hum, let me see" one. Intellectualization of the experience changes it and renders it impossible as an enlightenment. Further, because of the time and patience and devotion necessary to attain this feat, few Westerns have attempted it. So, to the Western mind, Zen enlightenment is obscure—from the impossibility of conceiving of it and the difficulty of attaining it.

However, we are informed by Zen masters and others who have attained enlightenment that, in this state, the Western conception of man versus nature is revealed as false and all is found to be in identity. The information concerning cataplectics and their means of controlling symptomatology tends to support the Zen view and to discount the traditionally Western way of dichotomizing man and nature. For, certainly, the electrochemical activity of a man's brain must be called a natural part of his total being, whereas his intellect is considered in Western culture an aspect of his godliness or nobility—that which "raises him above other creatures." The cataplexy information focuses down upon that miniscule but finite point where the two are one and, as in Zen, man and nature are in identity. The conclusion is inescapable that such dichotomies are artificial and false, that man and nature are one, incomplete when divided—just as two entities each called "half an apple" are still only "two halves of an apple" when combined and a "whole apple" is a different sort of thing entirely.

CHAPTER VI

The Uses of Humor

A question about humor already presented concerns the relationship between the participants in humor. What is the interpersonal contact between the persons smiling or laughing together? Ostensibly, they are enjoying themselves, are in "good spirits," congenial, "friendly." And, on a very superficial level, these words of description are quite adequate. They describe in a general, rather crude sense. But human behavior is far more complex, far more subtle; and "good spirits" is recognized as a shorthand for a myriad of other phenomena. There is much more to study regarding what goes on between those people.

Some naturalists have evolved a number of ideas about animals and birds and fish, etc., that are pertinent to this question about humor relationships. To study a subject, one has to have a point of view and some instruments. Information from naturalists has a good possibility of being as useful as that from any other presently available source. Just as truth can come from out of the mouths of babes, so it might from the pecks of a jackdaw.

For it is the pecks that are to be considered here—not only the pecks of jackdaws, but also the pecks of chickens, gulls, and other birds. And the pecks of dogs and cats and stickleback fish as well. This last sentence may seem to be nonsense. Everyone can see that dogs and cats and fish do not peck at all. However, they have behavior which is analogous within the frame of their own species to the pecking of Aves. The birds may be, with their beaks, the only creatures that can actually deliver a real peck. In many families of living creatures, however, there seems to be a type of activity which would likely be, if the organism had a beak, some form of pecking.

The fact that a general category of animal behavior that includes the pecking of Aves can be carved out with ethologic observation brings up a rather difficult but important question. Obviously the particular action of a bird tweaking its associate on the top of his feathered head, or elsewhere, is not the basic phenomenon. If a pecking type of behavior is found in other creatures who do not actually peck, then it must be quite apparent that a more fundamental purpose is involved. The question is inevitably raised regarding the functional aspects of this type of behavior.

It has been speculated and fairly conclusively demonstrated that pecking and homologous behavior in other species not equipped with oral horns is associated with establishing and maintaining social hierarchies. When two organisms come together, there is an innate tendency for them to attempt to determine which one dictates and which one is subservient. When many organisms are together, a much more complicated social structure is elaborated; but one aspect of this structure has to do with just such dominant-subservient relationships between the various individuals in the group. The relationship can be boiled down in its simplest terms to a question of who gets to peck whom.

It is already obvious that "peck" in this context stands for a type of behavior of a more general nature than is commonly designated by that verb. And it has been pointed out that this type of behavior is associated with establishing interpersonal hierarchies. Why is this behavior called "peck"? The reason for this nomenclature is historic, rather than philosophic. Some of the early and important studies of social hierarchy in animals other than man utilized data provided by observations of the pecking of fowls. Schjelderup-Ebbe, Tinbergen, Lorenz, Allee and his colleagues Masure, Guhl, and Cillias have all provided material and theories about this phenomenon.

A composite picture such as the following might be presented from their studies. In a colony of, say, twelve hens, there is a definite order as to who dominates or has the right to peck whom. This order is established through a process of trial and error, in which the various individuals square off in dispute at one time or another over food, territory rights, roosting positions, etc. The battling consists to a large degree of pecking at each other's head and comb. Hence, "pecking." After the battle, both winner and loser remember the outcome—apparently for quite a while (for there is much rigidity of structure in the hen society). And this means that henceforth the victor can feel confident of pecking the loser in any conflict of desires between them, for the duration of memory, and not being pecked back.

Consequently, among the twelve hens there is one who may peck at any others. She is the queen-despot and is the most dominant. Then there are hens who can peck all others except the queen-despot and perhaps one or two of their own social level. There are still others who may peck at all but those hens of the upper two classes, and so on until, finally, one poor hen lives in the group who cannot peck at any and gets pecked by all. Allee describes such hens as showing objective signs of fear, staying away from the others, eating at off hours, on constant alert. They may be lean, rumpled, and scarred. Occasionally the situation is so pernicious, Lorenz relates, that this lowly serf has to be removed from the colony to save her very life.

Actually, the prerogative to peck is rarely exercised by the dominant bird when two meet—for example, at the feeding pan. The dominant bird usually is content with threat, which consists of incomplete pecking behavior. All the movements up to the final tweak are performed, but by the time the beak is ready to thump down, the second hen is many feet away and the actual peck is not necessary. Pecks themselves may be of different intensity. They may be so light as to be only a metaphor of themselves. Or they may be so vigorous that the recipient of the blow goes reeling off.

Actual pecking is naturally confined to those creatures who are capable of such an act—those with beaks. There are, however, other ways of "pecking" when establishing interpersonal order. Analogous actions in other species might be the urinating habits of dogs, the growling and biting of coyotes and jackals, the paw slap of lions and domestic cats, the teeth ramming of social fishes.

Partly because of the widespread distribution of this phenomenon, partly because of its quality of automaticity, and partly because of other, more esoteric reasons, this type of behavior is generally regarded as inherent in the organism. It is felt to be an innate behavior pattern—inherited, passed from generation to generation through the germ plasm. It is considered to be a function of the organism intimately associated with the total idea of the nature of the organism, like the color of the eyes, the length of the tongue, the number of toes, the direction of usual movement. This behavior pattern must represent one of the very basic building blocks of interpersonal relationship.

The principle of social hierarchy is spread throughout the animal kingdom. In certain species—such as ants, termites, and bees—the hierarchy is so fundamental and inflexible that the individuals begin development at a very early age on one or another social level. An ant or termite on one social level has specific physical attributes which are common to members of that level and are different from homologous attributes of individuals born to other social levels. The case of a native California termite (Zootermopsis augusticollis) will illustrate the point.

A young termite (or nymph) of this species has several developmental possibilities. From the relatively undifferentiated nymph state, this termite can mature into either of three types of reproductive adult or into a sterile soldier. There is no worker caste with Zootermopsis, as there is with other genera of termites that exhibit more highly evolved social structures. The soldiers are conspicuously different from the others, with their long, armored mandible teeth. Their heads are larger than the heads of the other types and are dark and somewhat squarish. Their bodies are a light caramel color. No wings, actual or vestigial, are grossly evident. The first reproductive type has wings until swarming, when they fall off, leaving short thoracic wing stubs. The heads are round and flattened, with large black eyes. The bodies are light cinnamon-brown color. The members of the second reproductive type are different from those of the first in that their bodies are more similar to those of the soldiers in color and their eyes are smaller and pigmented. Short wing pads, only, are present. Still further variation is present in the third reproductive type. Termites of this type are without wing pads or wing stubs, and their eyes are very underdeveloped, being small and unpigmented.

There is considerable argument as to whether the type decision is made by the nymph's inheritance or whether the result is decided by various environmental factors. There is some evidence that both are involved. But whatever the mechanism for this type of development, the die is cast at such an early age that the termite's position in the caste system is associated with specific morphologic characteristics. Also, there is little movement from one level to another level for individuals in such societies. Theirs is an absolute caste system. And in such cases there is little "pecking" interaction between the various members of the different castes.

When such a rigid caste system is found, there is little likelihood of vertical movement, up or down. The individual is "born to the color," so to speak. There is little occasion for hierarchy duels to take place between individuals of different classes. Body structure indicates the respective privileges and obeisances. "Pecking" may take place between two individuals of the same level, but, relatively speaking, pecking is sparse.

At the other end of the spectrum of hierarchy is found a type of social structure which is very loose in its level organization. For the creatures demonstrating this behavior extreme, each individual action of aggression-submission stands sufficient unto itself. A king-despot may rule, because of his ability to defeat or bluff all others in the colony, but he may be defeated at any time by any member of his colony. If he is defeated by one member or another, he is defeated only by that individual and remains king-despot for the rest. Occasionally this arrangement results in the anomalous situation of having the king-despot pecking all but the most lowly member, who, in turn, can peck none but the ruler. The system is so fluid, however, that no one particular hierarchy remains in structure for long. There is much pecking and much actual dispute. Tomorrow's battle may have a completely different outcome from that of today. This is a very incomplete sort of caste system. The two extremes (rigid and fluid) are roughly comparable to the caste system of eighteenth-century India as opposed to the caste system of America in the second half of the nineteenth century.

There are, of course, as with most sets of extremes, a large number of intermediate positions along the line from one extreme to the other. There are many societies which are structured neither so rigidly nor so loosely, but which have, rather, features representing different degrees of compromise with each of the two poles.

It is evident that there are certain benefits derived for the species from operation of each of the above described extremes, or of their modifications. In the

more rigid system, there is less battle; positions are
more fixed. There is less bloodshed and the race can
multiply more freely. In the opposite extreme, the
number of participants in the system is kept more limited because of the frequent fights and increased likelihood of fatality. But the quality of the stock would
seem to be enhanced in that only the fittest of the
colony will maintain their supremacy and prerogatives
to food and mates for any prolonged period of time.
These relative merits of each system are more than
theoretical; both systems, and their variations, are
found in Nature, apparently satisfying various efficiency
demands of the process of natural selection.

This peck-order concept has another characteristic
which has value for the study of Humor. That is the
automatism of the interrelationships. The automatism
of the very rigid type of hierarchy is self-evident.
Hormone influence, gene structures, temperatures,
proximity to the next organism—these and many other
specific environmental and hereditary factors have compelling, automatic influence on the organisms in this
system, directing it this way or that.

On the other hand, considering the loose-system
extreme, we find that there is more "free will" involved, in that the individual's position depends more
on the outcome of a fight in which it has been actively
striving, and less on entirely impersonal factors. Yet
there are certain strong elements of automaticity here,
too. Automatism is found in the selection of combat
as the means of settling dominance-submission problems. There is little evidence of variety of "choice"
for the organisms in these matchings. Forms of co-
operative or sharing behavior are significantly unusual.
The immediate responses to the outcome of battle are
also automatic. The defeated organism is defeated, and
very rarely will it occupy, nevertheless, the contested
territory, the desired roost, or the like. The victor
is just as automatically bound to its victory; once the
battle is won, the spoils are unhesitatingly acquired.
"The king must be king."

There are certain automatic aspects of the ascendancy conflicts that should be considered more fully here. Lorenz tells of observing two timber wolves in combat in an Austrian game preserve. One was finally overcome and lay on the ground, beneath the feet of the victor. Lorenz expected any moment to witness a massacre. This massacre seemed all the more inevitable because the vanquished wolf lay, inexplicably, with his vulnerable throat exposed, seeming to offer it to the fangs of the victor. But the severing of the jugular veins, the carotic arteries, the trachea—all of which were exposed by this posture—never took place. The victorious wolf seemed to be involuntarily frozen in position, unable to deliver the coup de grâce.

I have observed a similar interaction in other so-called wild beasts. A family of coyotes lived at the Fleishhacker Zoo in San Francisco. When my wife and I were observing them, there were five living in the same cage—a male, a female, and three pups of the female. We did not know whether the male was the pups' father or not. But we were surprised to observe that the female persisted in attempting to take meat from the pups, which were about three months old at the time. Her efforts were regularly foiled by the aggressive behavior of the male. He "pecked" her and she was thoroughly cowed. Whenever she started toward the pups and their meat, growling and with fangs exposed under her curled lip, the male would jump up and trot over to place himself between the female and the youngsters. He would then growl, or give a short bark, and snap at her head or muzzle. She would turn and hurry off. We watched this interaction for some time until suddenly the female didn't get away soon enough. She seemed to stumble, and lurched back on her haunches. We had seen a large defect in her upper lip and had assumed that this was the result of a previous battle with the male. Consequently we had every expectation of seeing bloodshed now, as the male closed in on her. But she, too, as Lorenz saw with the wolves, turned back her head,

exposing the soft, vulnerable underside of her neck to
the male's teeth.   He was suddenly arrested, as if
petrified, and then turned back to his resting spot.
The female remained unharmed.

Such behavior is not restricted to wild creatures,
but can be found with domestic animals as well. Some
friends of mine had a large German shepherd dog,
whose playmate was a smallish beagle.   My friends
kept the shepherd penned up most of the time when
they were at home.   The beagle was allowed to run
free, and he frequently paraded around the yard, making a great show of his freedom.   This behavior apparently irritated the larger dog, and occasionally, when
out of the pen, he attacked the beagle.   These attacks
could easily be distinguished from the play that otherwise took place between the two dogs.   There was
dominance to be reaffirmed.   The beagle seemed to be
terrified of the savage onslaught. He was always bested,
ending up on the ground looking for all the world like
a roast pig awaiting the start of the banquet. He would
then turn back his head, exposing the neck, and the
bigger dog would be stopped precipitately.   The shepherd seemed to resent this control from within and
frequently would bring his jaws together several times
with a clicking of teeth.   He was even observed on occasions to turn his head up and jerk his muzzle back
and forth as if shaking an imaginary beagle caught between his jaws, to break the victim's neck.   But he
was never able to bite—frozen, as it were, by his own
inherent, automatic controls.

Lorenz points out, with regard to the positions that
trigger such inhibition of aggression, that usually the
positions utilized by defeated organisms to save their
life are those which would seem to expose them most
dangerously to being slaughtered.   Vital and poorly
protected body structures are presented for violence.
Lorenz states that the area and body structures presented are those very ones toward which the majority
of the killing attacks of each species are spontaneously
directed.   Furthermore, he refers to instances of special

"signal organs" being located in these vital areas—whether to mark the target or to underline the message, it is not clear. An example of the signal organ was the bare red spot on the head of the young water rail. When presented "meaningfully" to an obvious superior, the spot turns a deep red hue. It would seem that interpersonal communication by this type of submission signal is of very ancient lineage, for a special organ to have evolved over the centuries.

Further examples of automatic behavior are offered by other species. Certain fishes are automatically affected in their fighting by the distance from home. The farther away from his nest a male European stickleback has chased a rival male, the more hesitant and insecure he becomes. And the closer he is to his nest, the more fierce and aggressive he is. This response to geography results in the neatly working-out of various kingdoms, in each of which one stickleback reigns supreme and outside of which he tends to be frightened and quite humble. If two male sticklebacks are living as neighbors, there will be a line somewhere between them which indicates the point at which the attacking fish is so far away from home that his opponent, only so far from his nest, matches his aggressiveness and is able to prevent any further advance.

Automatic, too, are the threat and fight postures of cats. The threat posture entails a fluffing-up of fur, an arching of the back, an elevation of the tail. The cat seems to rise on its toes and may bounce around stiff-legged, looking like some kinds of spiders. On the other hand, a fight posture involves crouching with shoulders and head down and extended. One paw is usually raised and the face is "contorted into a fiendish mask." These postures may be learned from mother or older siblings, or they may be passed from generation to generation across the germ plasm bridge between this hour and the dawn of life—this argument is not settled. The important point is that the postures are involuntary, reflexive. They are the automatic responses to external and internal environment. And the creatures we have examined here—wolves, coyotes, dogs, fish, cats, hens, and termites—are but a few of the possessors of automatic traits. Automaticity runs through the spectrum from the totally automatic over-all structure of the termite colony to the separate automatic gestures and responses in individual hierarchy battles. By necessity, the automaticity labels the behavior it characterizes as innate, instinctive, or, with a term usually used in reference to humans, <u>unconscious</u>.

Can there be any doubt that the principle of social hierarchy applies to humans as well as to the lower forms of life? We have kingdoms, empires, states, families, gangs, clubs, unions, business and professional organizations. All of these contain various levels of ascending dominance or descending submission. All have a leader or leaders, vice presidents or captains, associates or lieutenants, etc., all the way down to that woebegone butt who, in the U.S. Army at least, may be called "yard bird"—with more reason than poetry.

And is there any doubt that "peck order" is relevant for humans as well as other creatures? We are immediately reminded of that sad and pitiful image— the henpecked husband. We are also reminded of the many cartoons and stories based on the following theme: wife pecks at husband over morning coffee; husband, who is president of large bandage manufacturing company, pecks vice-presidents at office, 9:27 A.M.; vice-president pecks office manager, 10:00 A.M.; office manager pecks sales manager, 11:32 A.M.; sales manager pecks salesman, 1:06 P.M.; salesman pecks office clerk, 2:50 P.M.; office clerk pecks stockman, 4:21 P.M.; stockman goes home and pecks wife over evening coffee. And what of the seating protocol for diplomatic banquets, or the arrangements for a political convention? Who shakes hands with whom? Who says "sir" to whom? Who gets to sit in the front seat when the family goes driving? Who sits next to the window? Who gets the drumstick from the roast chicken? Social

hierarchy and aggressive-submissive interaction relationships can be easily seen to play a very definite and
important role in the lives of humans.

The recognition of human social hierarchy and aggressive-submissive interactions, and the knowledge
that these phenomena usually operate in an automatic
or unconscious way—these make possible an interesting conjecture about humor. It is possible, in this
context, to consider smiling and laughter as being
(among other things also, of course) unconscious, nonverbal communication signals specifically having to do
with social hierarchy and aggressivity-passivity, with
humor as a territory in which these interactions can
be carried out. Smiles and laughter are then seen as
inherent methods of communication; from this standpoint they are automatic and, similarly, the reactions
to them—like the freezing reaction of the wolf in response to the exposed neck—are automatic. (Again, I
beg the question of whether these activities are inherited or learned.) Smiling and laughing can be considered as members of a large body of nonverbal messages
that are used by human beings to communicate specifically about peck order matters. Smiling and laughter
are analogous to the wolf's exposed neck or the plant-
ing down of the cat's paw, etc.

With this conjecture about humor and its attendant
laughing and smiling as an experimental model, examine
various humor phenomena and consider how they might
be fitted into the pattern. Beforehand, I hasten to affirm my belief that smiling and laughter are more than
just communication signals about dominance-submission.
They are multidetermined. To limit one's study of,
for example, textiles to consideration of the colors
alone does not deny other textile qualities such as material, weave, usage, pattern, weight, chemical composition. In limiting the scope of this chapter, there is no
denial of the existence of aspects of humor other than
those considered here.

When the idea was first conceived that smiles and laughter might function, in human communication, as messages about dominance-submission, I thought that they would be signals of surrender, that the appearance of either in a human relationship could indicate to an outside observer that a contest had been going on—perhaps unconsciously—and that the individual who smiled or laughed had been bested. The Virginian's "Smile when you say that" immediately came to mind. This thought carried with it the implicit suggestion that such a signal might also automatically act as a stimulus for a "sparing reaction" in the victor. A smile, for instance, would "freeze" the winner as he were about to annihilate his defeated adversary.[1]

---

[1] Studies in interpersonal psychology suggest other peck order phenomena that might play rather crucial roles in human affairs. Interpolation of data drawn from education for combat in military services, experiences of concentration camp victims with their Nazi guards, and gang-warfare folklore leads one to the conclusion that, unlike wolves, coyotes, and dogs, man automatically reacts with aggression to signals which seem to indicate submission, instead of being frozen into a "sparing reaction." Man reverses the structure obtaining on lower levels and, when the gladiator has fallen, requesting mercy, the thumbs turn down in spontaneous response. (One wonders what a cringing dog thinks of a master who reacts to his submission signals in a manner opposite from that which his instincts have prepared him for and kicks him. We could speculate at great length about the effects of this nonverbal communication inversion on man-dog or man-wolf relationships and the like.)

Awareness of the aggression-response phenomenon might possibly throw some interesting light on some of the perplexities of international politics. Munich becomes the surrender signal. Appeasement is the wolf on his back with neck exposed. But the human, constituted differently from the wolf, is impelled by this signal to rush in, with blood boiling, for the kill. The sign of defenselessness and a wish for peace and fellowship, the indication of "no war," is just the very message that precipitates the attack.

The problem of the warmongers, the group that desires war, is somehow to draw from the intended victim such a submission signal. The victim must be inveigled into presenting the olive branch. Think of the pre-World War II speeches by

(Footnote continued)

Hitler. His predominant theme was "we want peace." (But the theme was not presented in a submissive way. Hitler was able to avoid becoming, at that stage of the game, a victim.) The logical answer to "we want peace" was "yes, we too want peace." And then there was Munich, "peace in our times," the umbrella, etc. But what followed was radically different from what one would expect, if one only read the words. Munich was just the ingredient needed (from our nonverbal aggression-submission standpoint) to raise the German people into such a blood lust that they were all too willing to rush into "Hitler's war." When "we too want peace" is said, then the fight is on. (Of course, there are other psychologic phenomena that go into the preparation of a nation for war, but this approach seems to have something to it.)

The aggression-response phenomenon pertains to more prosaic matters as well as to top-level muckamuck. There is the problem of the lawsuit gambit. A rather commonplace experience is for a person to have some difficulty, in which someone else is injured through his own carelessness, result in a lawsuit against the first person by the injured party. Many people have been shocked and surprised by this sort of sequence happening in their lives. A colleague of mine visited a supposed friend in the hospital. The friend had fallen in the home of my acquaintance and had fractured a leg. The injured party was very embarassed about the accident—which was his fault—and apologized profusely for the inconvenience it caused. My colleague hastened to assure him it was perfectly all right—accidents will happen—and, to emphasize the words, visited the man in the hospital, bearing gifts of roses, sweetness and light. The next day my colleague had a lawsuit on his hands, demanding financial responsibility for the injured party's care.

Another similar episode involves a friend of mine who ran into the back end of a stranger's car. The stranger had neglected to indicate his intention of stopping at a stop sign and my friend, who was driving slightly above the speed limit, could not avoid hitting his auto. Both parties were clearly outside the law, and one would expect that everything would be handled between them quite properly and carefully. The stranger was very apologetic about his greater share of blame for the accident. My friend was very cordial also, admitted that he was partly in the wrong, and protested the stranger's self-recriminations. The next morning my friend was awaken by two policemen who had a warrant for his arrest sworn out by the stranger of the night before. My friend had made a passivity signal and was attacked for his pains.

This whole area requires much further study.

As data were examined, however, it became obvious that my original thought was too naive. And I became chagrined to think that I had imagined it to be as easy as all that. A far more complex picture began to take form. Smiles and laughter should be thought of as having a much more complex role in peck order battles than that of simple surrender messages. They can be surrender messages, but they can also be recognized as announcements of victory, weapons of offense, weapons of defense, signals of avoidance of battle, signals of preparing attack. In brief, they take many roles in a peck order contest. Smiles and laughter are involved with communication during these contests.

Among the humor phenomena that recommend themselves for examination are some items of folklore. Folklore—that which is traditional in a culture—is frequently quite revealing with regard to that culture and the people who composed it. Often enough it contains brilliant insights into human behavior. Folklore has generally passed many tests of time. At the least, it implicitly tells us some of the ways in which people of preceding ages have thought about humans and human activities. Since these people were humans and since their thinking about humans and human activities was itself a human activity, this folklore, even though the explicit content of its material may be deceptive, leads us implicitly to knowledge about human behavior. Cultural anthropologists regularly utilize folklore as an important tool in studying groups of people. Freud owes folklore a large debt for many vital clues in his studies of the psychology of man.

Folklore may consist of customs and beliefs. It may be represented in ancient stories and ballads. It may be embodied in wise sayings or proverbs and in figures of speech. The folklore of our Western civilization is extensive and is manifested in many forms. In the study of smiling and laughter certain figures of speech are of interest. There are many traditional figures of speech concerning smiling or laughing. Some

of them are: a disarming smile, a winning smile, weak
with laughter, a warm smile, a smile of friendship, a
sickly smile, die with laughter, "smile when you say
that," a triumphant laugh, a fiendish laugh. These are
enough to present the point. In almost all of such figures of speech, the idea entities which are brought together in the figure are those of smiling or laughing
and of some sort of contest. The contest ideas are
not either victory or defeat exclusively; both are found.
There is both a winning smile and a sickly smile.
There is the triumphant laugh and the state of being
weak with laughter. The two exceptions to the rule—
the warm smile and the smile of friendship—may be exceptions more apparently than really. In relationships
of warmth and friendship a peck order is implied. For,
certainly, friendship is, in one sense, an adjusted and
balanced peck order relationship.

These figures of speech instruct us that two broad
ideas (combat and smile-laughter) have been unconsciously recognized as being linked. It may have worked
like this: years ago someone "turned a neat phrase"
utilizing this linkage. The phrase struck a chord of
deep recognition in a sufficiently large number of persons for the expression to win popular usage and traditional standing. Folklore involves just that. Some
ceremony or ritual or, in this case, figure of speech
is created—by accident or by a process of gradual trial-
and-error evolution, it doesn't matter which—and so
reverberates in the unconscious minds of enough persons of the culture that it is grasped tight and held
fixed in time. Folklore generally answers an inner
need, tells an inner truth. Only those products survive
that are satisfying to a large number of persons.

Further phenomena from a source rather similar
to folklore is found. Throughout the centuries philosophers and other people have been speculating about the
nature of humor. And, although the accompanying smiling and laughter phenomena have never before been
explicitly tied in with peck order operations, it has

repeatedly been suggested that humor represents some sort of struggle of personal forces. It was, for instance, stated by Plato that different forms of power, when feeble and unable to do harm, are ridiculous and to be laughed at. Hobbes proposed humor to be "a sudden glory arising from a sudden conception of some eminency in ourselves, by comparison with the infirmity of others, as with our own formerly." "Laughter comes," according to Baudelaire, "from the feeling of superiority over our fellow." Paul Carus was even more expressive about laughter in triumph. "Tendency wit," in Freud's concepts, frequently involves the idea of aggression against others. And so on. One scholar, Th. Ribot, divided the theories of laughter into two main groups—the incongruity theories and the superiority theories.

There are, also, theories of Humor concerning defeat. The "overcoming of disharmony" which is proposed by H. M. Kallen as the essential principle in laughter suggests the efforts of a defeated individual: "the object of laughter leads to redistribution, re-adjustment, harmony, not to real human loss." William McDougall states one type of situations exciting laughter to be "situations which are mildly unpleasant, except in so far as they are redeemed by laughter." And in a book by Max Eastman humor is presented as an instinct "for making the best of a bad thing," a "simple emotional mitigation" of failure.

These philosophers and others are in some ways like the old men of the tribe who sit before the fires telling the tribal legends; their philosophies have some lineage ties with folklore. For these philosophies also are products of human minds—minds, trying to solve the unsolved riddles, to describe the undescribed. Individual philosophies may not have the mass of support behind them that folklore does, but each is a concentrate of the reflections of many preceding minds.

There are many time-honored customs and ceremonies having to do with joking—or the process of presenting humor. Some of them have pertinence here. Some of these customs are suggestive of peck order relationships. Particularly, one is reminded in this line of thought of the orgies of joke telling which occasionally develop in social gatherings, when at some time during a party one of the group will say, "I heard a good one today. Do you know the one about. . .?" The theme is rapidly picked up. Everyone seems to have a joke to tell. A frenzy develops. Amusement usually runs high, there is much laughter, many good jokes are told. Each joke teller seems to be spurred on to tell his best, funniest story. To the outside observer, it frequently appears that a very vigorous competition is under way. In these sessions the ties between riddles and jokes are drawn much tighter. The joke teller seems almost to be deliberately trying to puzzle or fool (defeat the minds of) his audience. His success is marked by the guffaws of the listeners until the next person wants to try and asks, "Have you heard this one?" And it is interesting that if someone has heard the next joke and if that someone states that he has heard it—designating himself as immune to the snares of this story—some of the general hilarity is decreased. The group becomes less taken with that particular joke even though none of the rest of them have heard it.

Another curious point noted at humor orgies is that the host or hostess, or some older person or one of elevated position, is treated in a special way by the others present. These persons receive more praise and acclaim for their jokes—and less hilarity. They are deferred to in a way; the jokes of others are seldom referred directly to these distinguished ones, but the jokester usually seems particularly interested in their reactions. Such people as these often act as the arbiters in Humor sessions, and, as with the person who has "heard the joke before," their presence sometimes acts as a damper on the general mood.

It would be difficult to explain systematically all these little phenomena of interaction. But much light is cast onto them if we can think of the humor orgy

as being a peck order session. The joke teller is the
dominant one; the joke is his weapon; his laughter is
the sign of his victory. The audience is submissive;
their laughter is the sign of their acceptance of defeat.
With each new joke, the order changes somewhat. Sad
indeed is the lot of the one who knows no jokes or is
unable to amuse the crowd. I have observed an outsider become involved in such a competition and be
cruelly wounded. His jokes were funny, but no one
laughed, no one surrendered. Apparently, various members of the group had decided that they did not like
him and so would not submit to him. He soon became
the lowliest of the lot and, like Allee's hen, was a very
sorry sight. He was the peck order serf.

If a member of the audience has already heard the
joke to be presented, obviously the weapon is not very
sharp. The contest will result in the joke teller's
being assigned some intermediate position in the peck
order. As for those distinguished ones—host, elder,
or notable—whose dominance is already established by
prior recognition, they rule as benign despots over all
transactions. They are, so to speak, above it all.

The way of commonly presenting a joke—"Have you
heard this?"—implies a form of contest. If you have
heard the joke, it seems that there is no reason to
tell it. Actually, this suggestion is false. There are
many jokes which are as rich at second telling as at
first. There are even a few that are more enjoyable
at the second telling. But what is implied is that if
you have heard the joke and thus know the punch line,
there is no point in going on, because "I won't be able
to confound you. If you have heard the joke, my punch
line will not surprise you; it will not teach you anything new. It will not be demonstrated that I am superior to you."

This point is further emphasized by a study of
audience reaction. Despite the fact that everyone is
aware that certain stories are more pleasureful with
repeated telling, the audience will generally allow the
joke that has been heard before to be passed over for

one that has not—apparently being unwilling to examine
the possibility that this particular specimen is one of
those that improves with age. Or the telling of the
familiar joke may stimulate laughter of a restrained
degree as compared with new jokes. There is, in other
words, some correlation, insofar as the audience is
concerned, between height of amusement and level of
puzzlement. The more confounded the audience (or the
more they are "surprised" by the punch line), the more
hilarious the laughter. This rule is also demonstrated
when two jokes of a similar structure are told one
after the other. Because of the example of the first
story, the audience has some preknowledge of the nature of the second. They can partially anticipate the
climax. This repetition of structure frequently results
in diminished laughter in response to the second joke.

These observations very strongly suggest that in
any humor orgy the members of the audience automatically assume a submissive role and their pleasure is
directly related to the success with which they are defeated. Anything which produces a diminution of their
subjugation or a decrease of the jokester's dominance
also results in a lessening of laughter and amusement.

In considering humor and peck order as being related, I stubbed my toe on an obvious item—so obvious
that it was almost missed. The term widely used in
the English language to indicate the climax of humor
is "punch line." This term is of fairly recent usage,
but its origin is obscure. It may be derived from
Punchinello, the medieval Italian comedy figure. Or
from Punch, of Punch and Judy puppet shows. Or from
Punch, the English humorous weekly. Or perhaps from
the punch of fighting and boxing—the "punching" bag, a
"punch" in the eye. There are several other kinds of
punch also—a punch press or metal punch, for punching holes, and wine or rum punch, perhaps so named
for its "punch." As stated, the derivation of "punch
line" is obscure. But some light is shed on the matter
by the discovery that an accepted but less widely used

synonym exists.   This synonym is "sock line," and it
is usually restricted to burlesque jargon.   A connection
between a fighting punch and a joking punch line seems
thus to be tied more tightly.   A sock and a punch in
fighting are similar.   And the two together cannot refer
to any of the other possible derivation of punch line
(except the beverage punch that may have a "sock" to
it—but that in itself refers back to fighting again).

How did the punch of fighting lend its name to the
climax of a joke?   The climax could have been called
"lemon seed" or "tree top" or "wurbagle," for that matter.   But somehow "punch line" has fitted so well—in
the minds of the citizens—that it has persisted since its
conception.   This choice may be a contribution to thinking about the connections between peck order and
humor—the word "punch" (in fighting) fitted one of the
unconscious conceptions of what joking is and therefore
has continued on as a natural choice to connote the part
of the joke that represents the peak of aggression of
one person against another, wherefore a punch line is,
then, a blow, a sock, a punch.

One of the important joking ceremonies is tickling.
Laughter with tickling starts at an early age and continues on through the years of maturity.   The actual
physical act of tickling produces pain—as one may easily discover by attempting to tickle himself.   But something about being tickled by another person makes the
act more than merely painful and brings amusement
into the picture.   Tickling is, in the last analysis, an
attack of one person upon another.   A flesh and bone
dagger is jabbed into various vulnerable parts of the
victim's body.   He responds with laughter, squirming,
and usually requests for more of the same.   This relationship presents itself as one in which the dominance-
submission activity seems obvious.   If one tickles oneself, there is only pain.   No amusement is produced.
Another element that falls out—besides amusement—
when one tickles oneself is the element of contest.
There is no dominance-submission match then.   This

associated disappearance is suggestive. The concept of peck order in humor does not solve all the riddles of tickling. But rather, some of the riddles of tickling seem to indicate that the peck order and humor (as derived in tickling) are related.

A form of humor which resembles tickling and is even more graphic a representation of peck order is slapstick. This type of comedy almost invariably involves two (or more) individuals engaged in a supremacy struggle. Frequently, one contestant is presented as hopelessly outmatched, and much laughter is derived from observing his vain efforts to win out over his superior. Or, again, individuals are depicted in a struggle against a superior inanimate force or mechanism. Whatever the specific form, the general theme of slapstick is contest.

Practical jokes are another case in point. They, too, are obviously involved with competition. They represent, in their abstract structure, an attempt of one person or group to place another person or group in the position of being ludicrous—or of being ludicrous because inferior. They seem to be concerned with establishing peck order hierarchies. X ties a string to a purse, takes the string and hides behind a fence. Y sees the purse and grabs for it, only to find that it moves away. X has clearly outwitted Y, established his own supremacy. X will laugh in victory, Y may laugh in defeat. (But if the "play frame" is broken in one direction or another—by anger or by tears—the situation is no longer humorous and no one laughs. Peck order phenomena then call up other mechanisms. Pecking competition may continue—if Y sees and chases X— but humor has already fitted away and the chase does not interest us here.)

Up to this point the material has been familiar. Anyone could confirm these observations with his own experience. Most of us are familiar with the folklore expressions quoted and frequently use them. Customs of humor are easily observed. Tickling can be studied

at any time.   But the phenomenon which next recommends itself for consideration is of a radically different nature.   It goes back into a period of history that
is only imperfectly chronicled, and it belongs to a fringe
of human affairs that is rarely seen clearly or given
serious study.

There is a puppet called Punch who was derived
from Pulcinella (English, "Punchinello") who was derived from Pulliciniello who seems to have been derived
from polcino and who was related to Cucurucu who
seems to have been derived in turn from Cicurrus.
Quite an impressive lineage. If honest, it extends from
present-day marionette theatres all the way back to
about 200-300 B.C.   Punch, the English puppet, was
originated somewhere in the sixteenth or seventeenth
century, A.D.   Pulcinella, the Italian puppet, may have
had his origin as far back as the Middle Ages.   Pul-
cinello, the Italian commedia dell'arte stock character,
probably first appeared around A.D. 1500 and Pulliciniello some unknown time before. Pulliciniello is said
to be derived from a quaint figure, the polcino, a word
which was early Italian for the common chicken that
scratched in the farmyard.   Cucurucu is a name contemporary with Pulliciniello and appears to have been
another name for the same stock figure that Pulliciniello represented.   But Cucurucu apparently had an
ancestor named Cicirrus who was a stock figure of the
Atellan farce theatre. Cicirrus was also of the poultry
family.   He was presented as a "cock type."

Just as in certain families particular prominent
characteristics identify the various individuals as being
of the family, so Punch and his predecessors have common features which would seem to identify the family
line. An enormous hooked nose, a humpback, a prominent abdomen, a blustering and boasting nature, a love
for food and females, a mixture of wit and stupidity, a
timorousness, and a nasal squeaky voice—these are the
characteristics of Punch's line. Cocks are recognized
to have many of these same characteristics. Furthermore, Punch and his predecessors seem always to have

carried with them a symbol of their origin. Punch has a coxcomb ("a cap worn by a professional fool, like a cock's comb in shape and color.") Cucurucu wore cock's feathers in his hat. From those who have applied themselves to studies of puppetry comes the declaration that Punch and all his predecessors back to the ancient Cicirrus (whose very name is presented as being onomatopoeia for the cock's crowing) are connected with poultry. The Punch family is supposed to represent a burlesque, a travesty—in human terms—of the barnyard cock.

Punch is an extremely important and honored figure in the tradition of comedy. He is one of the very few "stock types" that have existed down through the ages of formalized comedy. He appears today; he appeared around A.D. 1500; he appeared in 227 B.C. From this fact it may be assumed that Punch reverberates to some eternal truth inside our hidden, or archaic minds. This grizzled survivor of man's younger days apparently embodies something we all must feel and must have felt through all these years. Punch portrays, upon his stage, something that we know inside ourselves. It is like a story Bateson tells of a visit with the late Dr. Stutterheim, government archeologist in Java. Stutterheim was speaking of the Garuda bird, a sacred mythological Hindu figure. (The bird is known in Bali as well as in other areas with Hindu populations.) He said that the Garuda came to Bali from India and found another Garuda bird already there. The point of the story is that this bird, which exists as a religious, folklore figure, represents the outward projection of an inner feeling or thought from the minds of men. Dr. Stutterheim meant that this inner feeling was found in Balinese as well as in Indians and so the Garuda bird recognized in Bali a spot where Garuda birds may live. Punch is like the Garuda. He is the outward answer to an inner thought, and that thought apparently knows not the "bonds of time and space" but travels with the human brain.

Punch, then, represents an important comedy element. He is said to be endowed with the characteristics of cocks. It is possible that he is not only the burlesque of poultry but also the burlesque of that which may be common to both poultry and humor—peck order. It would be difficult to explain his survival if he presented only a truth about poultry. But if he presents a truth about comedy—and humans as well, because comedy seems to be a human prerogative—then timelessness might seem more reasonable. Although the evidence is not conclusive by any matter of means, the possibility that Punch is an artistic embodiment of the peck order linkage between human humor and poultry is quite beguiling.

And what if all of this is true? If peck order is one of the important elements of humor and is one of the determinants of the relationships that exist between persons engaged in smiling and laughing together? If one of the multiple aspects of humor is related to the establishment of social hierarchy? Why, then, several points become pertinent. First, there is explanation for the many conflicting themes of aggression and submission patched onto the corpus of humor. The apparently inexplicable and contradictory philosophies would now begin to make some sense.

Furthermore, there is given additional vision of an item of human behavior. Peck order behavior, with its compelling automaticity and pervasiveness, plays such an important role in the social lives of lower creatures that it would not be surprising to find it in human affairs. It is certainly illuminating to recognize that human beings may react with social reflexes, may be bound in their dealings with one another by automatic peck order transactions. They do not develop physical characteristics of a particular hierarchical level—although we are reminded here of such phrases as "fat and jolly," "thin and sardonic"—but the underlying principle has application for man as well as the other creatures.

A chapter similar to this one could be written about the relationship between humor and human distance-nearness operations, or humor and human nurturing-education behavior, or humor and many other types of human behavior. Humor plays an implicit role in many of these, and obviously humor is more than just a system of communication signals about social hierarchy and submission-dominance problems. We might question the value of presenting a discussion that deals with only one portion of a much larger whole. But this discussion on social hierarchy can provide information of considerable importance for the over-all knowledge of humor. In a previous chapter, the discussion of the unconscious aspects of humor emphasized the extensive and inescapable bonds between humor and an individual's intrapsychic life. This investigation of peck-order has afforded a valuable vista of a role of humor in interpersonal communication. The presence of implicit roles of humor is re-emphasized and the tremendous complexity of what one might naïvely be tempted to regard as simple or uncomplicated—"It's just a joke"—is once again expressed.

Aside from the values of the foregoing, there is one further justification for the presentation of this chapter on humor and peck-order. The operation of humor in the network of communication, as message or signal or information, represents an aspect of humor that is essential for the discussion of the structure of Humor in the following section of this book.

PART   THREE

CHAPTER VII

Background for Theory

As was indicated several times previously, there have been throughout mankind's struggle for greater knowledge many attempts to discover the so-called essential nature of humor. An explanation of humor has been the golden fleece, and the nemesis, of numerous philosophic and psychologic works. There have been many speculations on the nature of humor; there has been little mutual agreement about it. Each proposal seems to be greatly or slightly different—but different—from all others. With, then, a desire to avoid compounding the confusion further, I shall discuss in this section the "architecture" of humor, rather than the "nature" of humor. (There is a comfortable difference between discussing why something is funny and describing the appearance of something funny.)

The original idea from which this book evolved was conceived during the process of research investigation of "the role of the paradoxes of abstraction in human communication." During the initial stage of the investigation the members of our research team began to feel that the point of view provided by our provisional research hypothesis—that the role of the paradoxes is a vital one—could lead to some new insights concerning humor. I chose then to direct my attention exclusively to humor. This book has resulted from the thinking pursued in these studies.

Because of the novel nature of our general research theories and findings, it is advisable to present at this point a detailed exposition of them before going on to discuss the information which they have contributed about humor. And, so that we may all be talking in the same language, a few clarifications are in order.

The word "communication" (as above, in the phrase "the role of the paradoxes of abstraction in human communication") is used here with a special meaning that refers to the new and growing body of knowledge called communication theory.[1] Communication, in this sense, denotes both intra- and interpersonal events, all aspects of the events that link an individual or a group with all other individuals or groups. This expansion of the word's usage is discussed at some length in the book Communication: The Social Matrix of Psychiatry, by Bateson and Ruesch.

The "paradoxes of abstraction" here involved are exemplified by those presented by Bertrand Russell and A. N. Whitehead in their philosophic work Principia Mathematica—particularly Volume I. Russell and Whitehead undertook to develop some clarification of what they called the "vicious-circle principle." Pursuant to this end, they examined a series of contradictions, or paradoxes. These paradoxes were described as being all based on the "fallacious" premise that a collection of objects may contain members which can only be defined by means of the collection as a whole. Russell and Whitehead called this phenomenon "reflexiveness" or "self-reference." They stated that such paradoxes as the ones examined were plagued by "vicious circles." Two examples of the paradoxes presented by them are (1) the Epimenides paradox and (2) the "class of classes which are not members of themselves."

Epimenides was a semilegendary Cretan sage of the sixth century B.C. He reputedly dwelt at Cnossos and was honored for his wisdom, his prophecies, and his poetry. Legend has it that he had a life span of

---

[1]See Chap. III.

three hundred years, of which fifty-seven were spent sleeping in a cave. In the collection of many wise and confusing things he is reputed to have said was the statement that "All Cretans are liars." At first glance, this seems to be a relatively innocuous expression of some personal prejudice or a commentary on some mis-adventure. Closer analysis yields an entirely different impression.

Taken at his word, Epimenides is also saying, "This statement that I, a Cretan, am making is untrue." Is he speaking truth or falsehood? The paradox is out-lined by saying, "If Epimenides' statement is true, it is untrue. If it is untrue, it is true." A circular para-dox is presented, for which there seems no solution.

"The class of classes which are not members of themselves" was prepared as another paradigm of the "vicious-circle principle." It was presented that, since it is possible to assume a class of classes which are not members of themselves, a seemingly insolvable paradox is precipitated. The classes which are not members of themselves ("themselves" being classes which are not members of themselves) must be classes which are members of themselves. If, however, they are members of themselves, ("themselves" still being classes which are not members of themselves), they must be classes which are not members of themselves. A circular paradox results.

An enlargement of the paradox can be attempted by utilizing specific, or concrete, items in the presenta-tion. Divide everything perceivable or imaginable into two classes. The first class will be the class of match-boxes and the second class will be the class of non-matchboxes. Among the many, many items that make up the class of non-matchboxes will be found the class of matchboxes. This is an apparently legitimate opera-tion, since we cannot, after all, light cigars and ciga-rettes with a class of matchboxes, only with the indi-vidual members of that class. We then find ourselves with two general types of items: (1) the group of class-es which are members of themselves, i.e., the classes of non-matchboxes, and (2) the group of classes which are not members of themselves, i.e., the class of matchboxes. The class of matchboxes is not a member of itself; it is a non-matchbox. But non-matchboxes are members of classes which are members of themselves. Consequently, the class of matchboxes should be a member of itself—a matchbox. But again, the class of matchboxes is one of the group of classes which are not members of themselves. The paradox builds up to the point that if the class of matchboxes is a non-matchbox, it is a matchbox. If it is a matchbox, it is a non-matchbox. There does not seem to be any resolution of the dilemma.

Russell and Whitehead presented several other paradoxes of this nature—the Burali-Forti contradiction, Richard's paradox, and others. They proposed that their "theory of logical types" resulted in an avoidance of these paradoxes. In brief, the solution consisted of setting a "hierarchy of types" which would exclude "illegitimate totalities." These illegitimate totalities are those which include, in their body, statements about themselves; they manifest "reflexiveness" or "self-reference." The theory of logical types stated the necessity of establishing a type order or hierarchy so that otherwise "ambiguous concepts" (hitherto included in the "illegitimate totalities" as that group of concepts or statements which renders the totality reflexive) can be determined as belonging to a different type (in the hierarchy) or, in other words, as belonging to a different level of abstraction.

For example, the statement "All Cretans are liars" would be of a different type from the other statements that lying Cretans utter. A class of matchboxes would be seen as of a different order from matchboxes. The class would be on a different level of abstraction from the matchbox. In the "hierarchy of types," it would be of a different type from the matchbox and the two would not be comparable. The immediate paradox is thus avoided.

The central research hypothesis—that the role of paradox in communication is of a vital nature—had its far distant origins in speculations by Bateson about the different levels of abstraction—implicit and explicit—present in communication. (You may start with an apparently simple statement—"The cat is on the mat." Indicate the level of this communication as the primary or denotative level. You can then build up a fascinating structure about this simple core. Metalinguistics, metakinesics, metacommunication, etc.,[2] enter the picture and you find, each on a different level of abstraction, messages about the primary statement, messages about the messages, messages about the messages about the messages, and so on.) Bateson suspected that the existence of these levels of abstraction must generate contradiction, paradoxes. And he also began to wonder whether these paradoxes were not, in some curious manner, essential or invaluable to communication.

One of the first phenomena studied was animal play. In 1952 Bateson and another member of the research team, Weldon Kees, observed two male Florida river otters at the Fleishhacker Zoo in San Francisco. Taking up a vigil at the side of the otters' home, they watched, took notes, recorded otter behavior on many hundreds of feet of motion-picture film, and, at several crucial points, entered into the otter activities.

The two otters lived on a circular concrete island surrounded by a moat full of water and reedy vegetation. In the center of the island was a wooden keg with a round hole bored through its side. The otters usually slept inside the keg. A diving board jutted out over the water from one point on the shore of the island. The otters used the board for sunning, as well

---

[2]Metacommunication" is defined as a communication about communication. See Communication; The Social Matrix of Psychiatry. "Metalinguistics" and "metakinesics," then, are linguistics about linguistics and kinesics about kinesics—or, linguistic communication about linguistic communication, and so on.

as diving.   The island and moat were located in a
large, shallow pit which was enclosed by a wire fence.
Bateson and Kees were stationed with their equipment
just outside the fence.

At first, the humans were disappointed with the
otters.   Bateson and Kees wanted to observe animal
play; they had chosen to study the otters because otters
are notoriously playful creatures.   But these otters
just lazed around all day, sleeping, eating, occasionally
grooming themselves (rarely each other, which seemed
strange), and occasionally oozing into the water for a
slow quarter or half turn about the island.   They did
not play.

They did not play until one day, desperate or inspired, one does not know which, Bateson tied a piece
of fishy-smelling paper to the end of a long string.   He
lowered the paper into the otter world and jiggled it up
and down.   Both otters saw it and came to investigate
the peculiar object.   They began to play with the paper
on the string and, soon, began playing with each other.
They rolled and pawed and wrestled, chased each other
round the island,   shoved each other into the water.
They had swimming chases; they dived at and after each
other.   In brief, they began to play.

Bateson and Kees found, during subsequent days
and weeks, that the otters continued to play with each
other.   Also, their general behavior had undergone a
change.   They were now more lively; they slept less
enthusiastically and studiously than before.   Instead of
sluggishly rolling off the side of the island into the
moat, they were diving smartly and briskly, and swimming round and round the island, chasing their tails
and spinning over and over while they swam.   They
took to grooming each other assiduously, so that their
coats began to shine.   Their physical appearance was
markedly improved.   Naturally, the observers were
pleased and ground out film, took notes, and talked
things over while these observations were taking place.
What they saw and recorded and talked about stimulated
the following lines of thought.

In animal play, there appeared to be, at first, two basic phenomena.

> (1) Animals are playing.
> (2) Animals are engaged in an interactive sequence of which the unit actions are similar to, but not the same as, those of certain other behavior sequences (fighting, sexual stimulation or copulation, nursing or feeding). In other words, an observer can generally recognize that the animals are playing (not fighting). What they are doing bears a resemblance to fighting, etc. It looks like fighting whereas it really isn't fighting. The assumption can then be made that play might be a metaphor for other, primary behavior.

The logic of this assumption is given strength by an occasional outbreak of pathology in the play system. Every once in a while it becomes impossible to differentiate between play and combat or other behavior. Play slips into another type of behavior. It is as though the resemblance between play and fighting, etc., became too strong and it became impossible for the participants to maintain the distinction. (This pathology also occurs frequently in human play.) This evidence suggests that some intimate relationship exists between play and fighting, etc., and that these behaviors are not two entirely independent phenomena, but rather are dependent on one another in some mysterious and intricate manner. We have chosen to think of this relationship as a metaphoric one, in which play is a metaphor of fighting, etc.

A further point can be made—that the participants in play (animals or humans) are able to determine that they are playing (not fighting, etc.). They must be exchanging some metacommunication ("cues," "messages," "cue-messages," "discriminating signals") that indicates one to the other, "Look, this slap—it's in fun, not anger." Somewhere in the process of play is the metacommunication that this particular episode is play, not a fight, etc. If play is thought of as a communication process, it must include metacommunication as part of the process. There is, in other words, communication about the communication. Play, then, is behavior which depends on the mutual recognition (through metacommunication—internal and external) that that behavior (play) does not mean the same thing as does that behavior (fighting, etc.) which play represents.

Three distinct items are thus involved in study of animal play. (1) There is the idea of a foundation behavior (fighting, etc.—reality, primary process, mood statement, life or death). (2) There is the idea of a metaphoric behavior (play—fantasy, secondary process, representation, just for fun). (3) There is also the idea of metacommunication (discriminating signals, cues, etc.—"This is different from that for which it stands," "This is play," "This is not real"). And with the recognition of the presence of such metacommunication, paradox enters the picture.

By their very nature, the metacommunicative "discriminating signals," etc., must be part of the play— that is, they must subsume the whole. Something about the play—implicit, unspoken, contained as an integral part of that play behavior—communicates the play message. These signals are, it is true, isolated as unique, specific, concrete action-events, for purposes of discussion. Theoretically, this distillation process is legitimate. The signals can be spoken of as voice tones, facial expressions, gestures, postures, etc. No matter how they are represented in philosophic context, however, they are, in operation, not just these specific entities. To isolate these signals is a violation of Nature. They are, in operation, inseparable components of the interactions about which they communicate. They are dependent, for their existence, for their content, for their structure, upon the situation they are both part of and signals about. They are one with the continuous ongoing behavior. And only by artificial and temporary maneuvering can the signals be distilled out of the play.

The existence and the necessity of such implicit signals have been recognized previously by various naturalists, philosophers, and psychologists. Bateson seems to have been the first to see that paradox is necessarily generated by the presence and action of these signals. In play, the message contained in a slap of a paw is "Don't believe this" ("It's not really fighting"). Because of the reflexiveness of the message, a circular-type paradox is generated. If one is not to believe the process (slap and message, etc.), one has then to believe (in obedience to the message "Don't believe" which also pertains to itself). If one believes, one is forced to "Don't believe." An apparently insolvable paradox appears.

The differences between play and fighting in this respect is obvious. In combat, the implicit message is "This is real, this is life or death." No paradox there. The message does not paradoxically invalidate and validate itself. A fundamental difference is present. In both instances the message subsumes the whole process—both "This is real" and "This is fantasy." But in the case of "This is real," there is no reflexive negation. It is as if Epimenides had said "All Cretans are honest." It is "the class of classes which are members of themselves." On the other hand, "This is fantasy" presents a completely different type of phenomenon, and paradox is inescapable. "This is fantasy" is of the same general order of things in the universe as "All Certans are liars" or "the class of classes which are not members of themselves.

Animal play has been considered up to this point. Now, I wish to point out that animal play and human play are not much different one from the other. The three basic items—foundation behavior, metaphoric behavior, metacommunication—are characteristics of both. The structure of the interrelationships of these three factors precipitates paradox in human play, as has been seen already in animal play. Also, despite the additional asset of a verbal language, which is sometimes utilized in a significant way, the human play metacommunication is essentially the same sort of implicit, nonverbal communication that appears in animal play.

Further research study left Bateson and Kees' otters behind in their watery home and branched out into many other areas. It soon became apparent that play is but one of many types of animal and human behavior in which paradox operates. Other such types of animal behavior include deceit, histrionics, threat. Paradox in human behavior is found in ritual, dreams, folklore, art, drama, psychotherapy, and humor. (It will be noted that most of these examples of paradox-centered human behavior are associated with pleasure or are generally considered to be "good" things.)

With expansion of the field of research came a further contribution to the understanding of the importance of the operative paradoxes. This contribution came from the information that all asymmetrical mental relationships are most readily conceived as intransitive.[3] It appears to be a characteristic of the human mind (perhaps based on its neuro-architecture) that, when it begins thinking about asymmetrical relationships, they tend to assume the intransitive form rather than the transitive.

As an example of how this tendency works, consider a biologic system. The pituitary-adrenal cortex endocrine system can be thought of in terms of an asymmetrical relationship. The pituitary releases a supply of adrenal cortex stimulating hormone, ACTH, into the blood stream. This hormone stimulates production of adrenal cortex hormones (compound F, for one). The blood-stream concentration of ACTH is one of the factors influencing the production, and blood-stream concentration, of compound F. The blood stream concentration of compound F, in turn, is itself one of the

---

[3]By the phrase "intransitive asymmetrical relationship" is meant circular relationships of distinct entities. This structure is exemplified as follows: P is a premise for Q, Q is a premise for R, R is a premise for S, and S is a premise for P. This sort of relationship is the alternative to "transitive asymmetrical relationships," in which the process is lineal. Example: P is a premise for Q, Q is a premise for R, R is a premise for S, S is a premise for T.

factors influencing the production, and blood-stream concentration, of ACTH. In other words, the amount of compound F that is in the blood stream acts as part of a chemical feedback mechanism and influences the level of production of the hormone ACTH that controls (in part) the amount of compound F produced.

Substituting the "if . . . then" of logic for the "if . . . then" of cause, a symbolic representation of the pituitary and adrenal cortex relationship could be set out as follows: pituitary activity is a premise for ACTH in the blood stream; ACTH concentration is a premise for adrenal cortex activity; adrenal cortex activity is a premise for compound F concentration; compound F concentration is a premise for pituitary activity. Or, $P_1 \frown Q_1$; $Q_1 \frown R_1$; $R_1 \frown S_1$; $S_1 \frown P_2$. In such a symbolic representation, there is an intransitive asymmetrical relationship. By thus setting up the relationship, we have followed the natural human tendency, but, in the process, have distorted biology. It is psychologically natural for humans to think of the pituitary-adrenal cortex relationship in the form here presented; but, in a biologic sense, the relationship more closely approximates the structure of the transitive asymmetrical.

Time and change enter the picture. We are disposed to think of $[P_1]$ influencing compound F production $[S_1]$ as being the same pituitary gland as $[P_2]$ influenced by that compound F production $[S_1]$. This is not the case. Effort is required for the one to maintain, even in his own thinking, that it is not the case.

The pituitary $[P_1]$ producing ACTH $[Q_1]$ which stimulates the adrenal cortex compound F production $[S_1]$ is never that same pituitary gland $[P_2]$ that is, in turn, influenced by the consequent compound F concentration $[S_1]$. The diagram is not: $P_1 \frown Q_1$, $Q_1 \frown R_1$, $R_1 \frown S_1$, $S_1 \frown P_2$. It is rather: $P_1 \frown Q_1$, $Q_1 \frown R_1$, $R_1 \frown S_1$, $S_1 \frown T_1$, etc. Time has intervened and pituitary $[P_1]$ is now pituitary $[T_1]$. But the human mind does not operate easily with the concept of time. As a matter of fact, only recently (comparatively speaking) has time been dealt with as one of the dimensions of the universe.

And the various theories dealing with time are still understandable, and perhaps even familiar, to only a very few people.

This discussion on the intransitive asymmetrical relationships is actually a discussion of the circular type of paradox—in another language.   Such circular paradoxes are intransitive asymmetrical relationships, and intransitive asymmetrical relationships precipitate such circular paradoxes.

A point that came out of this thinking was of great value to the research team.   Since it is very difficult for people to talk or think about asymmetrical relation-ships without involuntarily making them intransitive, paradox would then seem to be an important inherent characteristic of human mental behavior. If the struc-ture of the human brain is such as to make thinking in terms of intransitive asymmetrical relationships more likely than thinking in terms of transitive asymmetrical relationships, paradox would seem to be natural accom-paniment of human thought processes and is difficult, perhaps impossible, to avoid with the kind of brain that we have in our heads.

In connection with this discovery, information about the status of the paradoxes served to strengthen our impression about their role in mental behavior. White-head and Russell had proposed an avoidance of the "vi-cious circle" paradox. They presented, in their Theory of Logical Types, the principle that a collection of ob-jects cannot contain members which can only be defined by means of the whole collection—if paradox is to be avoided. Epimenides' statement "All Cretans are liars" cannot refer to the statement itself. The class of class-es which are not members of themselves cannot include that class as one of the classes.   Metacommunication, or communication about communication, must be recog-nized as an entity distinct from communication.   And so they constructed a hierarchy of levels of abstrac-tion.   The statement "All Cretans are liars" is of a different logical type, on a different level of abstrac-tion, from the other statements a lying Cretan might

make.   The class of classes which are not members
of themselves is made up of classes which are of a
different logical type from the items contained in each
class (consequently, the class of classes itself is of a
different logical type from its member classes).

This theory was without serious challenge until the
publication, in 1931, of Kurt Gödel's article "On For-
mally Undecidable Propositions of Principia Mathematica
and Related Systems."   At first the article had limited
distribution, but it has since come to be recognized as
a major contribution to the science of this era.   By the
use of an original and extremely complicated system of
reasoning, Gödel was able to demonstrate, among other
things, that the theory of logical types did not, indeed,
lay low the "vicious circle" paradoxes and that any attempt to establish a logical consistency in a complex
system was doomed to failure because of the precipitation of paradox in the reasoning utilized in attempting
to establish that consistency.

Whitehead himself lent authority to the Gödel objection in an address delivered at Harvard University in
1939.   In the address, which was published during 1941
as an essay entitled "Mathematics and the Good," he
briefly discussed the theory of logical types.   He stated
that "our only way of understanding the rule (of logical
types) is nonsense," that "this rule cannot be expressed
apart from the presupposition that the notion of numbers applies beyond the limitations of the rule," and
that, then, "the rule must be limited to the notion of a
rule of safety," while "the complete explanation of number awaits an understanding of the relevance of the
notion of the varieties of multiplicity to the infinitude
of things."

These statements have been interpreted as meaning—in the terminology being used in this book—that the
theory of logical types is itself reflexive.   It, itself,
constitutes an illegitimate totality, and necessarily so.
It is a statement about statements, and among these
statements are those which can only be defined by
means of the theory itself.   It breaks, in operation, the

rule that it creates, ("our only way of understanding
the rule is nonsense"). The rule, itself, was discovered
to generate a paradox.

Apparently, paradox is of such a nature that it cannot be excluded from human thought and communication.
Or rather, it might be better natural history to say
that the operation of the human mind is of such a nature that paradox cannot be eliminated. Paradox is
found to operate even in that theory (of logical types)
that is presented to avoid its operation.

The preliminary research suggested one more point
pertinent to the present discussion. That is: the presence of paradox seems to add much richness to life.
Mentioned so far is paradox in play, ritual, dreams,
folklore, fantasy, art, drama, psychotherapy, and humor.
These phenomena include much human creativity. A
large part of that which comforts and affords pleasure
in human life is encompassed in these categories. Paradox appears to be centrally vital in all of them. It is
not clear just how the never-ending oscillations of a
"vicious circle" paradox result in pleasure to the human
organism. But such would seem to be the case.

Consider dreams. Dreams have fascinated people
for centuries—perhaps since the dawn of man's present
way of using his brain, since those years long ago when
the frontal parts of the brain began to bulge and challenge the supremacy of the midbrain. Dreams are the
sources of great gratification to the individual dreamer.
Even terrifying dreams or nightmares represent attempts on the part of the sleeper to work out a satisfying solution to another, more distressing, real-life
problem. Many difficulties that would be too hard, too
cruel to face in the waking day are met and assuaged
in the real-unreal symbolic matrix of dreams. Mankind would be so much the worse for the absence of
dreams.

Paradox plays an important, central role in a consideration of dreams. When a person tells himself, "I

dreamt such and such last night," he is indicating to himself (or to whomever else he may be communicating with) that he does not believe that "such and such" really happened to him.   The cue-message involved in "I dreamt" means "it did not happen."   During the dream itself it is unusual for the dreamer to be aware that his dream activities are not real.   But after the dreamer awakes, there is usually little question in his mind about the unreal nature of his fantasy. If he still experiences in broad daylight some difficulty in deciding that "now is real," some concern is generally felt for his mental health.   As a matter of fact, just such dream-awake confusion is considered symptomatic of some types of severe emotional-disease reactions.

However, this problem in discrimination does not appear very frequently and only then under conditions of obvious stress.   One is usually able to indicate a difference between dream life and real life.   It is in this awareness of difference that paradox lies.   The dream life within itself might be called the primary process; there is very little metacommunication (or "metadreaming") going on while the dream holds the stage.   There is mostly mood and action, with little reflection.   Life awake also is much of a primary process, but there is a great deal of metacommunication as well.   There is much self-contemplation, reflection, abstraction, editorializing.   (The difference between dream and life awake has other features, of course.)

When, during life awake, a person says (or thinks) "I dreamt such and such," he is engaged in communication about what had seemed, during its reign, to be a primary process phenomenon; he is also engaged in metacommunication about the complete nonexistence of that very phenomenon.   "The dream was dreamed, but the dream didn't happen—it was both real and unreal." To say "I dreamt" duplicates the contradiction that is set spinning by "I am lying."   The two opposite, and seemingly incompatible, poles—reality and fantasy—are brought into juxtaposition and the paradox is precipitated. I suggest that it is at this point of the existence-

nonexistence of a dream that the dream's capacity for
satisfaction lies.   In that the dream is paradoxically
equivocal, it can provide easement of stress that appears in the real, unequivocal life awake.   The research
studies led to the decision that dreaming could not be
such without its quality of paradox.   Paradoxless dreaming would not be dreaming as we understand it; it would
be a state more closely related to insanity.   And, we
have a good reason to suspect, such a state would be
devoid of the comforts afforded human beings by dreaming.

Return to play momentarily as part of this development of the exposition of the richness lent to life by
paradox.   Play is an activity which has much value to
people throughout most of their lives.   It statistically
represents one of the most prevalent types of human
behavior.   Play is pleasant, desirable, valuable.   Play
depends on paradox for its essential structure.   Play
would not be "playful" if it were not for paradox.   The
paradoxical alteration or, rather, once-at-the-same-
timeness of real and unreal is what makes play what it
is.   "Let's play" creates a frame around a particular
series of episodes which are thus both actual and unreal.   Through play, as through dreams, paradox flavors
life with much that would be sorely missed.   And, again,
it seems that at the point where paradox operates also
lies an important part of the "fun" of play.

One final statement.   In the list of paradox-charac-
terized phenomena are such examples of representational productions as art, drama, and ritual.   (The word
"representational" is used here in its general, non-
classical sense.)   These too, like dreaming and play,
are important components of human life.   As a working
example, consider a specific—canvas and oil pigment—
painting.   There is such an object.   That is the first
point to grasp.   And now becomes relevant the philosophic question of whether a tree can fall in the forest
when no one is in the forest to observe the fall.   As

indicated by pointing out that there is such an object as a specific painting, the answer to this philosophic question depends, for us, on our reference center. If we are talking about a physical, molecular world (if we can talk in such terms at all), a tree does fall in the forest. If we are talking about the world in relation to what we are and know (and in certain important contexts, this is a much more relevant way of talking since we are, after all, talking), a tree does not fall in the forest.

Applying this argument to the painting, we find that the painting is then, like dream and like play, both primary and metaphoric. This duality is more easily understood in terms of dreams and play because their substance is process, not material. The primary and secondary are made up of more similar fabrics, whereas with a painting one has a body on his hands. I have attempted, by use of the tree-in-the-forest point, to emphasize the essentiality of humanity to the painting (aside from the fact that a painting has to be painted by a human in the first place) enough that the double life of the picture is clarified. Here is the painting— just like the tree—but if there is no communication between the painting and a human observer, the painting is a—well, just a "nothing"—like the tree in the uninhabited forest. There has to be metaphor. When we perceive the painting, we incorporate the duality. As the painting is an object, it is not a communication and therefore is, in the present sense, a nothing. As the painting is a communication (a perceived message, etc.), it is a something. Is it a something or a nothing? Is it real or unreal? In our perception, it would seem to be both. And so the paradox is precipitated—not only with nonmolecular, process sorts of things like play and dreams, but also with those sorts of things one can touch (but, of course, only in the sense of their process relationship to man, for there is no paradox in the painting-object itself).

I feel that in the precipitation of this paradox is held some of the pleasure of art.[4]   The tree in the forest is a fine thing indeed, "as is"; but the pleasure of it is found in its appearance in human mental behavior—which use, in the last analysis, precipitates paradox.   So with the painting.   And so with ritual, drama, etc. Ritual as a primary process behavior may be all very good and will get things done, etc., but it does the job more nicely and much more in terms of human value is picked up when it becomes secondary as well.   (As a matter of fact, ritual really is not "ritual" as the term is used unless it is both primary and secondary—and, consequently, real and unreal.)

It was through these general theoretic glasses that the structure of Humor was sighted. I wondered whether the foregoing principles could be applied to Humor. They were applied, and the result follows.

---

[4]I shall avoid the perenial question of why art is pleasing by stating that most probably the operation of paradox is not the only thing about contact with art that is pleasing. Our focus on the pleasure of paradox specifically avoids more general questions on the pleasures of art.

CHAPTER VIII

Humor's Anatomy

In the preceding chapter the architecture or structure, of Humor was discussed. What does this mean? Humor, after all, is a process in human behavior, not brick and mortar. It might seem strange to think of an ephemeral psychologic process in terms of lines and curves and corners.

Most human beings are predominantly oriented toward visual perception—especially, one might say with some justification, those individuals who would be most likely to read such books as this one. I was, myself, able to understand more fully the operation of paradox with the help of a circling-arm lawn sprinkler. Gregory Bateson asked me, "Which way is it rotating?" As we were far enough from the sprinkler for the mechanisms active in optical illusion to operate, I found it necessary to tell Bateson first "Clockwise," then "Counterclockwise," and then "It's alternating with each half turn between clockwise and counterclockwise." Finally I was forced by the evidence of my apparent vision to state that the sprinkler did not appear to be rotating at all, and that the two arms from which the two streams of water spouted were crossing back and forth, apparently through each other, so that one arm was first on the left and then the right, while the other arm occupied the opposite pole—all of this in a two dimensional plane. After I reached this peak of confusion, we walked up closer and found that the sprinkler was, in truth, consistently and without hesitation, rotating in the clockwise direction. Although I was not actually visualizing a material operation of, say, the Epimenides paradox, what I did see made it infinitely easier for me to comprehend paradox thereafter.

When humans speak of the architecture or structure of humor, or of other psychologic processes, we are speaking in terms that are helpful for our understanding, rather than affirming that humor has a body. If we were pigeons, humor could more easily be discussed in terms of the gravity constant—"g"—or if we were bees, we could more readily deal with humor by use of ultraviolet-light concepts. But we are humans and there is general, though unwritten and largely unconscious, agreement in visual terms. And so—"architecture."

I attempt here, with the use of the information presented in the preceding chapter, to picture the architecture of humor. Paradox is demonstrated to be so involved in that architecture as to constitute its very nature.

It has been impossible, however, up to this point, to determine why humor is funny. Freudian psychology has several ideas to contribute along this line, and the discovery of paradox in humor increases the knowledge. Even so, it is not yet possible to demonstrate the electrochemical events that are stimulated in human physiology and result in the subjective experiencing of humor.

With this important reservation in mind, let us proceed.

First, humor is play. Cues are given that this, which is about to unfold, is not real. There is a "play frame" (in the sense discussed in the previous chapter) created around the episode. The frame can be indicated by a voice quality, a body movement or posture, a lifted eyebrow—any of the various things people do to indicate fantasy to one another.

Just as nonverbal message in the animals have been described, so the same sort of thing can be found in human beings. Humans have a rich store of nonverbal communication devices. It is impossible to outline, at this early date in history, the complete repertoire of nonverbal devices used by man; we have not gained that much self-awareness as yet. Man is still too close to his predecessors in evolution to have more than a little inner awareness of his nonverbal cues. Still, by using verbal communication (as in such books as this) to discuss nonverbal communication, humans have been able to identify certain of their nonverbal cue-messages. It is possible that many nonverbal cues or messages are ritualized or commemorated in various of the traditional religious and art forms—the kabuki dances, ballet, etc.—and that future study in these areas will be quite rewarding. The new science of kinesics and recent advances in the science of linguistics have helped develop knowledge of nonverbal communication.

Although humans are still too primitive to be aware of every statement (nonverbal, particularly) to one another, the potentialities for self-awareness are greatly enhanced over those of the other animals. This position results from the human capacity for verbal communication. One might suspect that nine-tenths of every conversation is carried on by movements, expressions, voice tones, and other nonverbal elements; it is the remaining tenth—verbal communication—that represents the magic ingredient. For, by verbal communication, inaccessible to lower forms of life, humans can validate and elaborate. We are able to raise ourselves another level in the hierarchy of abstraction and, with visual perception concepts (and others) to aid us, we can increase self-awareness.

The process of conversing about communication has been referred to in previous chapters and called metacommunication. The point was made that animals are capable of metacommunication. But without verbal equipment, only nonverbal, the animal metacommunication is handicapped. The complexity of human communication allows it to far outstrip the communication of lower forms. (One may suggest that the fruit from the Tree of Knowledge in the Garden of Eden is an allegorical referent for this human gift for greater self-awareness through verbal metacommunication.)

With the animals, we find primary-mood signals, for example, and secondary-level signals about how the mood signals are to be taken. An example might be the bared fangs of the cat's rage, with all the secondary aspects that accompany and indicate that this cat is serious. And then there are signals given indicating that the secondary-level signals are of secondary level and to be regarded as being communicative about the primary-mood signals. Already, with such an interrelated communication mesh, is found a rather elaborate structure. But a jackdaw, say, does not have the elaborate symbol vocabulary that humans have and so is handicapped, stuck at its more primitive level of self-realization. The boon of verbal communication grants to its users the ability to transcend the limits of communicating about a communication. The human can communicate about the very process of communication, can devise communication theory, can engage in metacommunication, meta-metacommunication, and so on.

Human verbal communication is, however, not all unmixed blessing. Along with the great value of this ability to use verbal symbols there is a drawback. Humans can become distracted from the business of primary communication (which is nonverbal, to a major extent) by the words that are being exchanged. Many of us, for instance, tend to mis-identify newspaper headlines as informative and definitive statements rather than as seductions or the result of a declining circulation figure. We focus on the words and lose sight of the message. This is a mistake, and, in so far as it is pervasive, self-awareness is done a disservice. Despite such disservice, however, verbalization has undoubtedly been one of the crucial evolutionary modifications.

To return to humor—with the equipment provided by the peculiarly human usages of nonverbal communication, play frames are set around humor by nonverbal cue-messages.

Usually these frames are established at the beginning of the humorous episode. A wink, a smile, a gurgle in the voice will set the stage before the joke begins its evolution. The joker may communicate the message by the posture of his body or an almost unnoticed movement of his arm. His nose may wiggle; he may emphasize various sounds or frequencies in his voice. There are numerous possibilities. The implicit meanings of the total situation themselves may contain the cue-message.

There are jokes, however, which are not prefaced by such play-establishing cues. A practical joke is usually not amusing to its victim until near its end or after the joke is over. It may be funny during its unfolding to relatively uninvolved bystanders—but usually only if they have received the proper message that the episode is a joke. (It is certainly not funny to the bystanders if the play frame is exploded by real harm to the victim: if the gun is a real one, not a water pistol; if the tack is brass, not rubber. A great deal of horror can be generated by contemplation of the "jolly fat man" laughing over the prone body of his bleeding victim.)

The bystanders may be amused, and the perpetrator or joker may be getting a great deal of glee out of the whole business. But if the amusement becomes communicated to the victim before the climax of the joke, the humor escapes. If the victim becomes aware of the fact that he is a victim before the joke is brought to its peak, there is serious danger that the joke will be spoiled.

Usually the victim goes through the experience to the very end without consciously knowing that he is the butt of a joke, and without laughing. The "it's all a joke" message is then put over and the victim is able to find humor in the joke. Significantly, the joker and the bystanders who are all aware of the play frame may be laughing already. But not the victim. He perhaps may never laugh, may never find this joke which has been perpetrated against him humorous; but, after the joke is labeled as such, then humor is at least possible for him.

This evidence—that the victim of a practical joke is not able to laugh at the joke until it becomes a joke for him, until it is communicated to him that the episode is not "for keeps" and is "just a joke"—this, then, can be considered as particularly significant in emphasizing the importance of the play frame for the blossoming of humor. The victim will be without any conscious awareness of his role as the victim of a practical joke. Ideally, from the standpoint of the total humor potential, he will be the only one unaware of the nature of the situation. (A larger quantity of humor will be involved if observers are present and aware of the humorousness. What is a practical joke for the victim and the joker becomes a canned joke for the observers.) Similarly, the victim is the only one to whom the humor of the situation is inaccessible. He finds nothing to laugh about. The observers and the jokester may not laugh, it is true, for that would give away the joke, but they could, for they have shared the cue-message and know that "it's a joke." Sometimes they cannot contain their mirth and will spoil the joke by bursting into laughter. Finally, when the victim gets the message and the episode becomes a joke (i.e., the play frame is established), then he too is able to laugh.

Although most cue-messages are nonverbal, humans are not limited to nonverbal cues. The nonverbal communication is vastly predominant, but there are many verbal cues which, in their implicit content, serve as precipitators of play frames. A canned joke may be prefaced by the statement "Let me tell you a story," or "Did you hear this one?" or "I heard a good one last week," in addition to the nonverbal cues that are

emitted.   There are also rare instances of the situation joke or the practical joke being prefaced by a "Let
me tell you one" sort of statement.[1]

Humor, then, is an episode set off from the rest
of the world by a play frame: "What is contained here-
in is not real."   One is reminded of the Epimenides
paradox: "I am lying" becomes "This is not real."   The
joke's play cues (which are part of the ongoing process
and which appear at either the beginning or the end of
the episode or repeatedly all the way through it—but
which must be present) establish this process, which
they are an integral part of, as unreal: "This joke is
not to be perceived in the same way as those instructions for feeding the chickens."   The cue sets up the
situation as unreal, including, of course, itself as an
integral part of the ongoing process.   If the situation
is unreal, so is the cue-message, and the situation becomes real.   If it becomes real, so does the cue-message, and the situation is unreal.   A circular paradox
is quickly apparent.   Furthermore, as is suggested by
the examination of the practical joke, which cannot become humorous to the victim until the play frame (or
joke) is revealed, this paradox element is just as important in allowing and helping humor to be humorous
as it is necessary for play to be playful.   A part of
life is set aside; it is designated as being fantasy, as
not being real.   Paradox revolves all about it.   If it is
unreal, it is real; if it is real, it is fantasy.

---

[1]Cartoons have their own special frame establishers—some
verbal, some nonverbal.   In the first place, they appear in
magazines and newspapers.   This fact, in itself, causes the
specimen to acquire a particular complexion.   Then, they are
always set off from the rest of the material by a little lined
box or a wide blank border.   And they are frequently captioned
to indicate their genus, but this is not essential. The point
is: cartoons are recognizable as such by reason of the communication that "this picture is not of real life," or "is not a
real advertisement," by means of conventionalized message-
cues.   It is awesome, when one thinks objectively about it,
how few mistakes are made in cartoon recognition.

Viewed in this light, humor becomes a riot of paradox. Whereas the Epimenides story contains but one
paradox, each joke is usually studded with paradoxes.
A joke is usually never satisfied with just one play
frame—establishing cue (or paradox-setting cue). The
play frame is repeatedly reinforced in many ways
throughout the episode and, with each reinforcing cue,
an additional paradox is precipitated. An attempt to
outline or diagram the vast complexity of this paradox
system could only result in stunning the imagination.

Paradox is found within paradox, modifying the primary behavior, modifying each other, and, in modifying
each other, modifying themselves by indirection. One
is faced with the realization that this paradox-establish-
ing technique, so common in human life, creates a
labyrinthine world beyond ordinary statistical means of
measurement or description.

It will serve the cause of clarification to point out
some of the secondary paradox devices. Dialect is one
thing that is available. The humor-enhancing value of
dialect is generally recognized. There are Italian dialects, Scotch dialects, Jewish dialects, German dialects,
dialects of old men, "little morons," Russians, Irish-
men, and many others. Dialect is a common humor
technique and, in one sense, it re-emphasizes the "this
is unreal" quality of the episode. By definition, "dialect" refers to a type of speech which is not the same
as the speech of the joker. It is a type of speech which
is, in this sense, unreal. It is not part of the audience's
and joker's real world. Dialect generally is used in
canned jokes; but we often observe people who are playing practical jokes assume dialects, ostensibly to dis-
guise themselves. Even in situation jokes the climax
may be found to have been delivered in a voice tone
which could be thought of as "dialect" for the particular
persons involved. Caricature becomes pertinent at this
point and might be considered as closely related to dialect, in the sense that Groucho's false moustache and
Chaplin's large shoes restate the not-real quality of

their production. The limits of what is natural are exceeded by the extravagance of the peculiarity. This excess then serves to cue fantasy.

Another common humor-embellishing and frame-reinforcing device is the use of the "mock-serious attitude" in which one is offered an apparent reversal of the cues. This device is frequently used in the presentation of canned jokes and occasionally during the unfolding of a situation joke. It involves the joke teller's acting as one might imagine his grandfather would have acted, with the important difference that the grandfather probably never acted quite like that unless he himself were telling a joke in a mock-serious manner. In other words, this device is a vignette of play. One behaves in a manner that means something different from that behavior for which this behavior stands. There is really no difficulty in differentiating the grandfather from the joker. What results is a caricature of the worthy old gentleman. We can see that if the mock-serious attitude is a specimen of play, it is also paradoxical. Something in the attitude, perhaps a voice tone, indicates "This is unreal." The real-unreal paradox then appears.

Besides the mock seriousness being play (paradox) in itself, besides having its own internal (and artificially isolated) play frame, it necessarily acts, with regard to humor, in ways similar to other nonverbal cues—gestures, body position, dialect. It emphasizes by its nature not only that it is itself internally unreal, but also that the external situation (joke) and itself (the mock seriousness), as part of that joke, are unreal. It contributes to the play frame.

One further example of play messages will help to clarify this point. Often, during the telling of a canned joke or during the progress of situation humor, the participants—particularly the joker—will be seen to laugh or smile. Such expressions can usually be differentiated from the terminal laugh or smile which appears following the joke climax and is the humor response which all the preliminaries have been preparing.

This intercurrent laugh or smile is, no doubt, an expression of amusement, but it is restrained—it does not "give way at all its seams" like the laugh that is to come at the punch line.

If the intercurrent laughter becomes too boisterous or the joker is carried away in laughter by the as-yet-unrevealed humor, the joke is spoiled and the audience gets little humor from the episode. In other words, if the intercurrent laugh is more a genuine expression of amusement and less a fantasy message, the humor spills out and the joke is lost. It is important that the intercurrent laugh be cue rather than mood. It is secondary, not primary. The message that it indicates is "This is all unreal"—thereby reinforcing the play. It offers the suggestion "This is something worth laughing about, it's a joke, and you too will be amused as I am, when you hear the punch line." The cue laughter has this message that can reinforce the unreal nature of the episode.

These three examples discussed above represent a meager sampling of the myriad cue-messages—mostly implicit and nonverbal—presented during the unfolding of humor episodes. The richness of human communication is the point here.

Most of these metacommunicative cue-messages—the "reality-qualifying or discriminating signals"—are implicit, and all are internal with regard to the ongoing interpersonal process. The metacommunication is carried on by cue-messages which cannot be foreign and separate entities, cannot actually be distilled out of the situation, and are integral to the situation. It is important to re-emphasize this fact (which was so belabored in the previous chapter), because it is this self-referent quality of all the cues—verbal or nonverbal—which makes it inescapable that paradox be generated when these cues communicate about the processes of which they must be a part.

Humor is seen as play—an interpersonal process or communication which either starts out contained in a play frame or which is suddenly caught into such a frame from behind when the episode is at the point of termination. The play frame indicates that the process is unreal; the process is on a different level of abstraction from the laugh that follows it or from a fight to the death. It is a fantasy or metaphor for reality. And because of this playful nature, this metaphoric quality, humor must necessarily be paradoxical. We are confronted by the shimmering, endless oscillation of the paradoxes or "real-unreal." Humor becomes a vast structure of intermeshed, revolving rings of reality-fantasy, finite-infinite, presence-void.

But is it sufficient to say that humor is play? Will it be enough to recognize that a play frame sets off a joke, etc., from the rest of the world and creates paradox as a vital characteristic of the process? Perhaps so. After all, play is enjoyable and the source of a great deal of entertainment. Children, at least, laugh frequently during their play; they give many outward signs of amusement while playing. Adults, too, though not laughing as much as children, enjoy sports and many types of games. This observation would seem to indicate that play and paradox are enough to describe humor.

However, play lacks an element which apparently is vital to all that is recognized as humor. Play is an ongoing interpersonal process (communication), as is humor. It is metaphoric and paradoxic. But play and games have no punch lines. In all that is regarded as humorous in the adult human world, there is a build-up of the process to a climax or punch line.

The punch line is protean; it may be expressed in any one of the ways by which humans communicate. It may be words—or other sounds; it may be a movement or gesture, an expression, a situation. There are no rules about what punch lines have to be. But, punch lines are essential. Even a practical joke has to have a punch line which, although it may not be recognized as such at the time, provides the hook on which to

hang the laugh when the joke is finally revealed to be
a joke. It is not, then, paradox activation in the organism's brain by a framing procedure that alone iden-
tifies the ongoing process as Humor. There is more
to be said. Humor has a punch line.

A joke (of any variety) is play with a climax—a
process presented in a special context, engaged in with
a special mood, constantly oriented toward a particular
termination point (known here as the punch line). Apparently, it is just as essential that humor have this
climax as it is for humor to be surrounded by a play
frame. Consequently, several questions become appropriate. What are the main characteristics of the relationship between the joke climax and the rest of the
joke process? What are the dynamic consequences of
this relationship? And what happens to the joke process as the punch line is delivered?

Examine some characteristics of the relationship
between climax and process. First, the relationship is
a vital one. Process cannot exist without the climax,
and vice versa. Consider canned jokes—one can tell a
story without a punch line. But that is not humor. That
is just a narration—it may be interesting, but it is not
a joke.[2] One can tell a punch line without a story.
That is not humor. It may be madness or eccentricity.
But it is not humor. And these same judgments will
apply to situation and practical jokes. The relationship
is a necessary one.

Most persons who have speculated on humor have
recognized a particular quality about the punch line.
They have commented on the line's apparently incongruous, unexpected, surprising nature. Punch lines
seem to divert the stream of thought; they seem to

_____

[2]Some "shaggy dog" jokes seem to exist without punch
lines. The story goes on and on and finally ends with "not a
bang, but a whimper." There seems to be no punch lines.
Laughter results, however, because the device of trailing off
at the end of the story is in itself a punch line—a rather peculiar one, but a punch line nevertheless.

call for a switch of ideas and expectations. It has been argued by some that the funniness of humor depends on this incongruity, that humor brings about laughter through the unexpectedness of its punch lines. That this element of the relationship between climax and process is the essence of humor may be so. But there would seem to be more than simple incongruity or un-expectedness involved. The simply incongruous or sur-prising is not necessarily funny, even usually not so. From even a superficial study of the relationship be-tween climax and joke process it soon becomes obvious that much more is involved.

All this brings up the second question. What are the dynamic consequences of the climax-process rela-tionship? My answer is that the relationship is such as to create additional paradox and reverberate to the already established paradoxical nature of the humor-presenting situation. The punch line is so related to that ongoing process of which it is actually an integral part that a further circular paradox is precipitated—a "vicious circle" paradox which, however, specifically concerns the humor content rather than the total situa-tion and which is itself contained within and is itself affected by the encompassing play frames. In other words, the punch line is related to the rest of the humor episode through the actual content-materials of both these elements (the punch line and the rest) and in such a fashion as to create paradox specific to this content. Also, it is additionally related to the total joke situation inasmuch as it is dependent on the al-ready established (or to-be-established) paradoxical na-ture of that total situation.

In the examination of the evidence for these con-clusions is found the answer to the third question—what happens to the joke process at the delivery of the punch line. Consider what happens as the punch line is de-livered. For this exposition, we need examples. A canned joke recommends itself as a preliminary ven-ture. (I shall, in this, follow the time-honored custom of examining a very dull joke. This tradition is perpetuated in deference to those of us who enjoy humor and who are occasionally amused. After all, it would be a species of brutality to study those jokes which may be dear to the heart of one or another of us.)

A man enters a bakery shop and orders a cake baked in the shape of the alphabet letter "ess." The next day he calls for the cake, opens the box to see it, and complains, "But I meant a capital ess (S). This is a small ess (s)." The baker apologizes and promises a capital ess for the next day. When the promised time arrives, the man returns to the shop, receives his cake, opens the box, sees that the cake is truly an "S," <u>and eats it.</u>

What has happened? Someone has "told a story." The content of this story is fantastic—not only fantastic in that a man orders a cake in the shape of the letter "S," but also in that the content is the content of a "story." The joke was designated as such from the beginning. By using the noun "joke" to identify the episode described, I designated it as a humorous story— untrue, play, a verbal game, unreal, fantastic. I threw a play frame around the episode and precipitated para- dox. Moreover, it is fantastic also, because a man orders a cake in the shape of the letter "S." Fantastic because he is given a cake in the shape of the small letter "s." Fantastic because he refuses the "s" cake. Fantastic because he insists on capital "S" cake. Fan- tastic because he gets an "S" cake. Fantastic that he eats the cake in the shape of the letter "S." But not at all fantastic that he eats a cake. After all, what are cakes for?

Again, viewed in another light, viewed in the light that the whole story is fantastic because it is a story, the content is not fantastic. In other words, the joke content may be considered as not fantastic at all—if one remembers that it is the content of a joke. It is not fantastic about the cake, about the man's refusing the cake once and then accepting it. It is not fantastic about his eating a cake shaped like the letter "S." But

it is utterly fantastic—in the context of joke telling—
that the man should eat the cake. The world of fantasy,
of nonsense, is concerned with other things. And just
as cakes shaped like an "S" are fantastic in our workaday world but to be expected in the nonsense world,
so is it fantastic in the context of nonsense that a man
eat a cake (or, for that matter, do anything else of
such a practical nature).

There are, then, two ways of describing this particular joke. Its content may be thought of in terms
of the "everyday world" and will appear to be fantastic
until the reversal at the punch line. Or the content
may be considered as sensible within the context of
humor until the introduction of the fantastic by the
punch line. And it is possible to have these two seemingly opposed orientations actually coexistent only because the whole episode presents paradox. It is somewhat like watching the perceptual oscillations in the
optical illusion of the Necker cube. The cube is presented as a game. If the Necker cube were presented
as a flat diagram (if one were instructed that "it is a
blueprint for the laying of a tile floor"), no visual oscillations would be possible. But it is presented as a
cube—the "picture" of a solid, three-dimensional object.
A game is constructed about the possibility of seeing
the cube two different ways. Optical illusion is called
up, and one is invited to play. So with the joke.

We have a story about a man and a cake. Fantastic, perhaps, but regarding the content of a joke it
doesn't really matter whether that content makes sense
or not. In one context, the story may be nonsense; in
another context, the story may be quite sensible. One
of the characteristics of humor is that questions of
sense and nonsense are suspended. The play frame
changes the rules of reference in such a fashion that
these rules are beside the point.

It is important, however, that the content of the
joke be recognized as the "reality" of the moment.
One ordinarily does not think of dreams as reality.
When one is dreaming, though, the dream usually

becomes reality for the time. And so it is with humor.
No matter how fantastic the explicit content of a joke
may seem, it is the reality of the time it occupies.
These are the words we hear or the movements we
watch. Consider the Necker cube. No matter which
way the optical illusion presents itself, there are the
lines on the paper. Do with them as you will in your
mind's eye, the lines are there as an external, perceived entity.

(In the interests of brevity and simplicity, I am
comprising with the principles of rigor and using "reality" to refer to that crude but practical distillate of
perception which is generally agreed as making up the
world: "that which has objective existence—not merely
an idea.")

In the terms that are being utilized here, an explicit story about a man and a cake constitutes the
reality of the time being. Along with this explicit
"reality" is grouped a host of implicit accompanists.
We have seen in earlier chapters that the body content
of each joke is accompanied by innumerable implicit
themes, both conscious and unconscious. Much of this
implicit material is doomed to remain forever implicit.
But it is the art of the punch line of the joke to snatch
some of this implicit material from the world of Shades
and project it into the workaday world or, in other
words, into reality.

Until its delivery, the content of the punch line has
been an implicit ghost. It has been an unreal accompanist to that which was presented as reality. Freud
called it the "unreasonable," the "unacceptable," "something new." Reich described it as instinctual, asocial,
grotesque. In general, it may be said that what was
being described is the implicit, unconscious and conscious, that which exists by virtue of suggestion or association, stimulated in the world of ideas by the explicit joke reality. A vagary in the unreal world of
dreams and shadows, this implicit content remains without objective actuality until the punch line is delivered,
when it becomes explicit and is precipitated into the
world of objects.

The process is similar to thinking "I'm going to drop my glasses" and then suddenly being confronted by the perceptual "real object" of oneself grasping for the glasses as they fall to the ground. Other occasions during which the implicit may become explicit take place during psychiatric therapy, during dreams, during play, in the telling of myths and legends, in the theatre—at times when fantasy is used as a material in the construction of reality. But life is lived in such a way that this carnification of implicit ghosts occurs most commonly in joking.

During the unfolding of humor, one is suddenly confronted by an explicit-implicit reversal when the punch line is delivered. The reversal helps distinguish humor from play, dreams, etc. Sudden reversals such as characterize the punch line moment in humor are disruptive and foreign to play, etc. (Only in psychotherapy is this sort of reversal operation compatible with the general structure of the experience.) But the reversal also has the unique effect of forcing upon the humor participants an internal redefining of reality. Inescapably, the punch line combines communication and metacommunication. One receives the explicit communication of the punch line. Also, on a higher level of abstraction, the punch line carries an implicit metacommunication about itself and about reality as exemplified by the joke. In our joke about the man and the cake, the implicit ideas about people eating cakes become explicit communication at the delivery of the punch line, this implicit-now-explicit punch-line material becomes a metacommunicative message regarding the joke content in general (as a sample of communication). In this reversal of content, what seems to be reality can be presented in terms of what seems to be unreality. Content communicates the message "This is unreal," and in so doing makes reference to the whole of which it is a part. We are thus again confronted with the paradox of the negative part defining the whole. Real is unreal, and unreal is real. The punch line precipitates internal paradox specific to the joke content, and stimulates a reverberation of the paradox generated by the surrounding play frame.

To make more vivid what has been noted so far, borrow some phenomena and concepts from Gestalt psychology and apply them to the present exposition. I refer to the general area of figure-ground relationships and in particular to the attention-alteration aspects of figure and ground. In a still-life picture, say, a vase stands out as the figure against all the rest within the picture frame—the ground. When the viewer ceases to attend to the image of the vase and attends instead to the banjo beside it, the vase joins the ground and the image of the banjo jumps out of the ground to become the figure. In the rendering of a musical composition, the same is true. A listener might attend to the figure of the bassoon against the ground of the violins and the timpani. Again, there can be an alteration of attention, and the timpani become the figure and the violins and bassoon the ground. This principle can be applied to lexical material. At this moment, this word is the figure, with all the rest of the printed page as the ground. Another moment, and another figure has appeared, with a different ground.

For each perceived item that sets itself up in the perceiving organism's brain as the immediate figure, there is related material that is perceived though not attended to and hence is the "ground." Further, the figure and the ground are within the frame of interrelationship (the vase is the figure against the ground of the rest of the painting, the painting is the figure against the ground of the wall on which it hangs, the wall is the figure against the ground of the room, the room is the figure against the ground of the house, etc.).

The extension of this concept from the area of sensory perception to the area of cognative perception would seem to be a legitimate extension, though perhaps somewhat deviant. Such an extension would involve the indication of a communication (perhaps

originally sensory) as figure and the indication of all
conscious and unconscious themes implicit to that communication as ground.   One could indicate a particular
dream-symbol, perhaps a house, as the figure and all
the conscious and unconscious associations and determinants of that symbol as the ground.   In applying
this schema to jokes, one would find the spoken, written, or acted joke as the figure and all of the accompanying conscious and unconscious themes stimulated in
the minds of the audience as the ground.

Consider the story about the man and the cakes as
a figure.   Implicitly, with this particular figure—a story
about a fussy man and two absurd cakes—there is a
ground.   One of the elements of this ground has to do
with that purpose to which people usually turn cakes—
that is, eating.   But, comes the punch line, and the
figure is no longer the figure, the ground is no longer
the ground.   The punch line produces a sudden change;
the ground becomes the figure and the figure becomes
the ground, as in looking at the Necker cube.   The
punch line activates a reversal of reference.

So far, this example seems to present a rather
simple picture, closely related to optical illusions, but
because of the added fillip provided by the self-inclusive
and self-referent nature of the implicit metacommunication of this reversal, much more is involved.   With
an optical illusion specimen—such as the Necker cube—
one is usually presented with the specimen as an exercise in optical illusion, a reality so composed that alternatives in perception are possible.   "Reality" includes
this alternativeness.   If this possibility of perception-
alternation is not included as a component of the reality of the optical illusion exercise, we find that what
has been merely interesting and curious, now becomes
a source of humor (provided that the proper play frame
is available).   What is usually presented as an optical
illusion—the Necker cube, for example—becomes, instead, a practical joke.

Although the figure-ground concept is useful in discussing joke structure, obviously more than just figure-ground reversal is involved in humor production. When a joke is presented (in contradistinction to when an optical illusion is presented), the reality of the presenting situation does <u>not</u> include the "ground" which is implicit to the content "figure" of the body of the joke. The ground is certainly there, but on higher levels of abstraction than the object-reality figure of the joke content. For a visual figure-ground exercise, vase, banjo, and the rest of the painting are all explicitly there—receiving different emphasis of attention at various times, but representing the same level of abstraction.

With a joke, however, one is presented with the object-level "thing" in the body of the joke and the implicit is given no concreteness—it is left on higher levels of abstraction and is elevated beyond object reality. It is left, that is, until the delivery of the punch line, when it is precipitously made explicit. There is a vital difference between the nature of the figure-ground relationship in perceptual experiences and in a joke. That difference is played upon when the joke's punch line is delivered. And the more-abstract is made less-abstract. Or, in our other terms, unreal becomes real.

The inevitable consequences of this difference in figure-ground relationships between nonhumorous perceptual experiences and jokes is that in the joke, when the ground becomes figure, paradox is generated. The Epimenides statement "I am lying" can be considered to be a figure until it is pointed out that this specific statement has a more general meaning, which was previously implicit-ground but becomes figure when pointed out or made explicit (and in the process, denies itself).

The implicit ghosts (or "ground") of a joke become explicit upon the presentation of the punch line. The figure composed previously of what was "real" communication becomes a figure of what previously was

"unreal" communication.   The <u>negative</u> part defines
the whole: paradox.

It is now possible to pass on to an even more be-
wildering complexity.   This complexity has to do with
the effects of the bringing into relationships of the
"internal" or content paradox and the "external" or
play-frame paradoxes.   Throughout the telling of a
joke, there have been frequent messages sent out to
emphasize and potentiate the over-all paradoxical nature of the episode.   The presence and operation of
these messages have been examined.   The oscillation
between real and unreal throughout the joke as a consequence of these "external," "total situation" paradoxes
has been observed.

Because of this oscillating, there is the peculiar
result that it is possible that, on one level, the reality
("figure," "thing") in the pre-punch-line part of the
joke be either the explicit story (the story about the
man and the cake) or, until now considered the unreality ("ground"), the implicit idea (eating a cake).   In
another way of speaking, the paradoxical nature of
humor makes it possible for any one element of a joke
to be seen, in the broad context of the whole specimen,
as both reality and unreality.   The magic of humor
provides a shimmering moment at the punch line when,
in the broad sense, real-unreal rules are suspended;
everything is figure and everything is ground.   One is
thrown into a strange and magical world, different from
all else we think that we know.

> "Footless sacred shadowy thicket, where a myriad berries
> grow,
> Where no heat of the sun may enter, neither wind of the
> winter blow,
> Where the Reveller Dionysos with his Nursing Nymphs
> will go."

Another joke can be examined in this study.   A
bald-headed man and his friend are standing outside a
tavern after having had a couple of drinks.   Just then

a seagull flies overhead and defecates on the bald pate. The friend is very much upset and exclaims, "Oh, that's awful!   Can I do something?   Let me get some toilet paper."   The bald-headed man rumbles, "Hell, no, he's probably a quarter of a mile away by now.

On superficial inspection, this canned-joke story seems to be an exact opposite of the one about the cakes.   The fantastic part of the content comes in the punch line.   It is quite reasonable that two men be standing outside a tavern and that one of them be soiled by a passing seagull.   It is fantastic that a seagull should use toilet paper.   In the other joke it was fantastic that a customer and a baker should go through antics over an "ess"-shaped cake.   But it was quite reasonable that a man should eat a cake.   But that, we saw, was only half the picture.   Since the customer and the baker were acting in a joke, their behavior was not fantastic and eating the cake, in that context, was.   In other words, because the episode was all a joke, the content could potentially be considered both fantastic and reasonable.   Similarly with this joke about the bald-headed man and the seagull, questions of sense and nonsense are beside the point.

What is much more to the point than "fantastic" vs. "reasonable" is that the joke, by being a joke, encloses itself in a play frame.   A play frame was established and paradox was generated.

Within this play frame, explicit material was presented.   If we can temporarily dissect in our minds the explicit material from its surrounding play frame, the explicit content can be identified as "reality."   As always, there is also the unreal world of implicit themes that accompanies the explicit.   A bald-headed man is the victim of a defecation.   And implicit to every defecation is a defecator.   (After all, the theory of spontaneous generation was discarded some decades ago.) The reality presented is that of an unfortunate man and his friend and bird feces.   Off in the mists of abstraction is the implicit orifice.

That is, until the punch line is delivered. Then the implied defecator is made explicitly real. Implicit becomes explicit. In the context established above by temporarily dissecting away the play frame, unreality become reality. Metacommunication about the nature of reality is delivered by virtue of this explicit-implicit (figure-ground) reversal. "This is unreal" comments upon itself. And again paradox is generated.

Having been able to see (1) the external play-frame paradox and (2) the internal content paradox, put them back together, as they actually exist in Nature. The joke than becomes an immensely complex structure of paradox in which the mutually referent statements "this is unreal" and "this is real" are combined in such a vast number of ways that each simple joke—such as this one about the man and the seagull—presents a variety of structures that might require months for a human analyzer to diagram. And, of course, in constructing a series of diagrams to illustrate the variety of ways the many paradoxes might be interrelated, violence is actually done to the essence of the phenomenon.

The material being discussed in this chapter is of such an order of complexity that it would be very useful to be able to present a diagram of the "architecture." My efforts to devise such a diagram have so far always run into the difficulty that it commits an important violence to the essence of this humor structure to put it on paper in lines and arrow, etc. One can draw a diagram of one-half of the explicit-implicit picture. And one can indicate, by drawing the other half, that the first drawing was only, in fact, one-half. One can indicate, by codifying information on the margins of the diagrams, how the diagrams fit together, and one can describe the nature of their relationships.

I have, however, as yet discovered no technique of illustrating the instantaneous simultaneity created in paradox. Nor have I found a method of diagraming in a finite way the complexity of self-reference active in the paradoxes of humor. One would be faced with an infinite-regress problem such as was found on the old

Dutch Cleanser can.   Finally, it seems impossible to
picture the flavor of elusiveness given to "reality" during the process of humor.   How can one depict "not
something"—which concept is, after all, a vital concept
for paradox.   Even to leave a blank in the diagram to
indicate "not something" (or "unreal") is to do a violence to the notness of the concept.   (It might be that
some type of mathematical symbolization can be applied
to humor to give an accurate representation of its structure.   The use of advanced mathematics, however, is a
skill beyond my capabilities. I shall rest in the thought
that this book may stimulate persons with such mathematical skills.)

So much for canned jokes.
Inspection of a situation joke should reveal the same
general structure.   As a specimen use an interaction
which appeared during a psychotherapy interview con-
ducted in another phase of our research project.   The
patient had been discussing his difficulty with aggression, observing that his taboos against aggression made
such behavior, when it appeared, much more violent
than it otherwise might be.   He was, in other words,
ruminating on the irrationality of the "all or none" principle in this particular behavior.   He spoke of an episode, pertinent to this problem, which took place in his
childhood.
During his early school years, he was walking in
the street with a group of other children when they
came upon a crippled bat.   The other children were
fascinated by the fluttering creature. Our patient, however, was so upset by the sight of the maimed creature
that he seized a large rock and hurled it at the bat,
crushing and killing it.
He then went on in the interview to speak of further examples of the same sort of difficulty. Perhaps
half an hour later, discussion having turned to totemic
animals and how the "all or none" aggression operates
in periodic feasts on these totemic animals held by
various primitive peoples, the therapist held up his

ring, on which is engraved a bat-wing silhouette. The therapist explained that the bat was the heraldic or "totemic" animal for his family and went on to say, "Our ancestral animal is the bat and I thank you for putting one out of his misery." This statement was followed by a spontaneous burst of prolonged laughter on the part of both patient and therapist.

Despite the fact that this exchange took place in a highly specialized setting, it is similar to the sort of humor that appears often in everyone's daily life. Two (or more) persons are engaged in communication. They are suddenly amused by some item of content, which may seem completely humorless to an outsider. The humor is derived from the ongoing process in which the particular individuals are participating. The therapist's punch line has all the elements which have been discussed as being essential to punch lines. It is vitally related to the content of the whole interaction. There would be no laughter without the punch line, and there would be no laughter without the ongoing process. Also, the punch line seems to be incongruous, seems to divert the stream of content, and so on.

Until the delivery of the punch line, the psychotherapy hour had progressed without any generation of humor over the specific material about bats. It can be hypothesized that, at the time of the utterance of the punch line, a nonverbal message was passed (perhaps a smile, or the wording of the comment, or a voice tone) that "this is play" (or, "this is unreal"). This paradox-setting message was vital—as in the case of canned jokes—for the possibilities of humor in the episode. Surely, if the therapist had stated "I thank you for putting one (of my ancestors) out of his misery" as a straight expression of serious emotion—anger, say, or gratitude—there would have been no subsequent laughter. The play-frame operation is as vital for situation jokes as it is for canned jokes. (In this situation joke, as in many practical jokes, the reality-qualifying cues appeared at the terminal stage of the process.

Many situation jokes, like most canned jokes, are preceded by these cues, or have them appearing early in the episode.)

Within the surrounding real-unreal paradox, there is a relationship between joke content and punch line that is identical with that of the canned jokes we have analyzed. The climax does the same things to the whole process. The climax calls attention to a ground that has existed throughout the entire period and that is implicit with reference to the verbal content of the episode. In this example, the climax calls attention to the nature of the relationship between therapist and patient—a nature which has been implied throughout the preceding minutes. The punch line results in a derangement of the previous orientation. Figure (discussion about "all or none" aggression) becomes ground, and ground (communication about the relationship between therapist and patient) becomes figure. And, because of the now evident, essentially paradoxical nature of the whole episode, "all or none" aggression is both figure and ground, as is the relationship between therapist and patient. Or, in the other way of speaking, both are real and unreal at the same time.

Again in this example, several essential elements are present in the structure of humor. There must be both body and punch line. The punch line must be so related to the body as to present a different content from that which is presented in the body. A reciprocity of content must be arranged. At the delivery of the punch line, that content which has been unreal (unspoken, implicit, apparently without substance) becomes the reality, and the definition of reality is exploded by the question of what is unreal. In the process, the statement "this is unreal" appears, with the consequence that content-paradox is generated. This all must be surrounded by a play frame or circular paradox which makes relevant again the questions of "What is real?" and "What is unreal?" And the punch line, in presenting its paradox, will vibrate the outer paradox.

There are some situation jokes in which but one person is amused and which would seem, on superficial inspection, to violate the specifications just set forth. For example, consider the person who, in the street, is highly amused by another man's chasing his hat as it is blown away. This sort of episode is frequently presented as an instance of humor and, although I have never experienced or observed such an episode, it should be considered.

It may be presented that this is a joke amusing only one person and that therefore there is no communication between persons about play, paradox, levels of communication, etc. There are no messages passed between the man chasing his hat and the one laughing at it all. There is no "this is not real." It is reasonable, however, to assume that for the laughing spectator the man chasing his hat has become a symbol. In other words, despite the fact that no communication may exist between the spectator and the man chasing his hat, who may not even notice that he is observed, there are two (or more, but at least two) phenomena present for the spectator. On one hand is the perception of a stranger chasing his hat. On the other hand is a symbol for something entirely different. The man chasing his hat becomes a metaphor—as well as being a man chasing his hat. He becomes the spectator's boss who has just lost his head and is running after it as it goes tumbling down the street. Or he becomes the spectator himself, punishing himself for having been surly with wife and children that morning. Or something else. (It is the richness of our fantasy that constitutes one of our most important reliefs from tragedy and makes it possible to laugh at so very much in the world.)

There are, of course, others watching the event who may not be amused, who may not laugh. They may rush to help the man chasing the hat, they may say "What a shame!" In such case, the man chasing the hat is no metaphor. He means nothing more than an unfortunate man chasing his hat. The unamused spectator is moved to primary action.

There is one further point. The man chasing his
hat may become a metaphor in a spectator's mind and
yet the spectator may not laugh; he may weep. The
metaphor may involve tragedy rather than amusement.
At this point the play frame again becomes important.
Tragedy is not play. With this tragedy, there is metaphor in the air, but paradox with play frame is not in
the air. On the other hand, for the spectator who
laughs, it is reasonable to assume the internal existence—in the laugher's mind—of a play frame self-created
and internally communicated.

This internal existence is argued for by an important point. If the man chasing his hat were to stop
chasing it and draw himself up into a posture of dig-
nity, it is very likely that the amused spectator would
no longer be amused. A self-created play frame would
be destroyed and the amusement would no longer be
possible. The spectator, for reasons usually known
best to himself, has chosen to see as play this particular episode of a man chasing a hat and had, inside his
cranium, communicated a play cue to himself: "It is
not real, it is a joke." Not five minutes ago, he may
have seen another man chase another hat in another
street and wept. This time he laughs. Five minutes
hence, he may see a third man chase a hat and again
weep. But, for some reason, and this reason is always intimately connected with the symbolic content of
the episode for the spectator, he has laughed at this
particular episode. He has snared the episode—in his
own mind—in a play frame.

Having discovered the development of metaphor in
the laugher's mind, we are now again in the position
to recognize the presence of the internal content paradox. To do so, it is merely necessary to accept
the explicit-implicit relationship of a metaphor and that
which it denotes. This relationship revolves on the
axis suggested by Bernard Berenson when he stated,
"Artistic feeling is born of the meeting of the life im-
prisoned in a work of art with the life within the man
contemplating it. 'We must look, look, look until we

live the painting in front of us, and for a fleeting moment, we identify ourselves with it.'" And then, for that fleeting moment, the metaphor is that which it denotes—or, in another vocabulary, a punch line is delivered—and that which it denotes is the metaphor. One's definition of reality is forced into a new position. The familiar playing with the levels of abstraction is found; the negative message of the process defines the whole, itself included.

So much for situation jokes. Consider now those types of humor designated as practical jokes. And, as stated previously, this genus includes those jokes which, though contrived and artificial (like canned jokes), are also related vitally to the ongoing social process. There are many specimens of wit and comedy, much of slapstick humor, many amusing puzzles and conundrums, all of which fall into this category.

A well-known example is the old "April Fool" prank of tying a string to a purse and then placing the purse on the sidewalk, as if dropped. The joker takes the other end of the string and hides. When a victim sees the purse and reaches for it, the joker pulls the string, yanking the purse out of the victim's grasp. A variety of subsequent actions is then possible.

Examine this joke. It is obvious, as before, that a variety of actions subsequent to the yank of purse are possible. The victim may be amused or not. The joker is likely to be amused, but there is also the possibility, too, that he may not be amused. The victim may spot him and start after him or may throw a rock. Or the tragedy of the victim's not getting this fine purse full of money may be so overwhelming—if the victim sits in the street and weeps—that the joker is seized with grief and remorse and solemnly swears "Never again!"

If, however, the message "This is play" is sent to the victim—by the nature of the situation, the movement of the purse, or some other integral part of the ongoing process—and he is "in a mood" to play, there will be

general amusement. Even if he rejects this communication, but does not destroy the play frame for the
joker or whatever audience is around, amusement for
these other persons is possible.

A further alternative exists, that the joker becomes
engaged in internal communication that "this is serious,
this is real life, etc.," and amusement is completely
banished. The reality-qualifying signal ("this is unreal")
is of vital importance to this type of humor as well as
the others. The activation of paradox, as a result, is
inescapable.

It may be instructive to consider initiation rites of
hazing at this point. Hazing could be defined as a practical joke without a punch line. Certainly there is a
close relationship between hazing and practical jokes.
Many of the same activities are found as the content
material of both. There frequently seems to be a similarity of purpose in the hazer and in the practical joker.
However, these two are different in that there is no
punch line in hazing. There is, in addition, another
important distinction.

Often, in hazing, the activity begins with a spirit
of glee, interlarded with laughter and smiles. As the
procedure progresses, the laughs and smiles disappear
and the whole spirit undergoes a gradual change to the
serious side. Frequently, it all ends with the hazee feeling out of sorts—discouraged, frightened, angry, dis-
gruntled. Or, he may complete the experience with
another sort of serious feeling—that of being inspired,
elevated, or exalted. This sort of reaction is, of course,
foreign to a practical joke.

An essential distinction between hazing and practical jokes lies in the device that would seem responsible
for this difference of emotional reactions on the part
of the victim of the joke, on one hand, and the hazee,
on the other. The message that is offered throughout
the process of the hazing is "This is serious." Frequently, each laugh that might escape from the hazee
during the early stages of hazing will bring the reward

of a punishment. In college initiations, paddling may be one of the hazing activities. The paddling is usually found to become more strenuous if the hazee is "defiant" and is laughing or smiling during the experience. Or, if the hazing is treated as a "joke" by the hazee, he may be returned to the beginning of the gantlet to repeat the experience again and again until he takes it "seriously." Compare this situation with that of the practical joke, where the object is laughter and the creation of humor—and the message "This is unreal" established the play frame.

Return to the purse on a string. The play frame is established. The rest is more difficult. It would seem that the same internal structure and the same relationship between body and punch line (the "escape" of the purse) exists as in the other types of humor. The elements of the pattern, however, are by no means so clear as for canned and situation humor.

Until the purse actually moves, the victim has, ostensibly, one thought. He sees the purse as an interesting object. After all, he has voluntarily expended the energy to reach for it. It is not unlikely that it is not curiosity but desire for possession that has prompted his action. The victim has at this point an idea of acquiring property. Inherent in all ideas of acquiring something are ideas of losing something. (This truism could be extended to the thermodynamic principle of the conservation of energy—but it is probably not necessary to carry the argument that far.) When one is finding something on the street, there is implicit the fact that someone has lost something on the street. It would seem, then, that this punch line—the withdrawal of the purse—is the affirmation of reversals, taking its lineage from that which has been implicit in all that has preceded. The finder of the purse discovers that he has become a loser of the purse. Dreams become reality. Unconscious is solidified.

The punch line, in this joke as in those earlier discussed, presents as real an unreal accompanist of

that which was reality until the punch line appeared.
The purse was lying on the street; it was really there;
you could see it and, almost touch it. It must have
gotten there somehow. It didn't just grow out of the
concrete. There does not really seem to be anyone
around who might have lost it. The idea of its having
been lost is implicit in the whole episode of discovering it. It must have been dropped there. But what is
really happening now, at this moment, is I have found
a purse. Wisdom and experience state that someone
else must have lost the purse. That, however, is not
for oneself an actual occurrence at this moment. The
actual occurrence is one's discovering this purse—solid,
no mirage. And then the purse is jerked away. I have
lost the purse. The implicit becomes the explicit; the
unreal becomes the real. Fantasy takes on a fleshy
look and assumes the garb of the workaday world. The
reversals begin to spin again. The paradox of real-
unreal pertaining to joke content is again prepared and,
when the episode is revealed as play, the whole paradoxical complexity is precipitated.

Another example of the practical joke is even more
complicated and presents a particularly rich study. It
starts with the joker saying, as if beginning a canned
joke, that he has heard a good story.

"Did you hear the one about the bride and the gas?
As this bride is walking up the aisle on her father's
arm, she suddenly leans over to him and says, 'Oh,
Daddy, it's awful! The gas—I can't stand it any more.
What shall I do?' Her father says, 'Wait until you get
near the roses!'" Then the joker, in an anxious manner leans over to the listener-victim and asks, "Did
you hear it? Did you hear it?" Seemingly he is
inquiring as to whether the joke is already familiar.
The listener-victim, believing that the joker wants to
know whether he has heard the joke before, says "No."
Whereupon the joker states, "Neither did I—I was in
the back of the church." And what was interpreted as
being a canned joke turns out actually to be a practical
joke.

This is a particularly complicated joke, but it is especially revealing with regard to our hypothesis. At the delivery of the punch line there seems to be a sort of double-explosion kind of humor. One recognizes a neat trick (or practical joke); also, one is amused by the punch line content. The whole episode starts out in the climate of "This is play." The episode is presented as a joke. "This is untrue" activates the paradox frame around what is to follow. The story unfolds; then, apparently, the frame is broken by the question "Did you hear it?" The joker seems to have become serious. He seems to have stopped playing, momentarily. He indicates, just as does a purse lying unattended in the street, that "this is real." His metacommunicative cues are signaling a positive message ("this is real," as opposed to "this is unreal"). In other words, the paradox frame seems to be fractured at this point. Then, however, comes the punch line. The paradox frame is revealed to have been continuous and vital throughout. (After all, if the question "Did you hear it?" is not included as part of the joke material, there is no sense—at least, no humor—to the joke. If the question continues to be perceived as an element outside the paradox frame, the story becomes inexplicable.) The question is then exposed as being included in the same real-unreal oscillation as the rest of the content. Instead of having the paradoxical nature of the episode reaffirmed by reversal in the punch line alone, this process is extended through two stages of the joke. This is one of the complicating, and also humor-potentiating, features of the joke.

The content paradox which is precipitated by the punch line ("Neither did I—I was in the back of the church") is associated with the figure-ground association of the smell and sound of released flatus. The initial content presents the idea of smell alone, with the father's reference to the roses. The idea of roses suggests their fragrance which, in turn, suggests the other odor in the joke—the flatus. But it will be (and is, for the mind of the listener) the fragrance of the roses

that will hide the odor of flatus.   The listener attends
to the roses and forgets the other.

Then, with the use of the content of the seemingly
disconnected question ("Did you hear it?"), the idea of
hearing flatus is introduced by the punch line.   The
hidden flatus again puffs onto the scene.   That this
joke is a practical rather than a canned joke depends
on this point.   For if the question "Did you hear it?"
were presented as part of the ongoing joke, rather than
as a return to seriousness, the joke would be a canned
joke, but a very poor one, perhaps even humorless.
"Did you hear it?"   "No."   "Neither did I, etc." will
stimulate few persons to laughter.   So, then, the idea
of hearing is (all unaware, because of the externalizing
of the question) focused on, and content figure-ground
relationship is set into reversal movement by the punch
line.

Perhaps because the climax of this joke is drawn
out in this fashion, the importance is emphasized of
both these essential humor qualities—the paradox-play
nature of the episode and the content paradox activated
by the punch line.   Through the apparent breaking-in of
"This is serious" or everyday reality (in the use of the
question), there seems to be a cracking of the play
frame.   If the frame were allowed to remain open at
the question, by a punch line that did not refer back to
the seemingly disconnected question, the joke would not
be a practical joke.   It might be a rather dull canned
joke.   The punch line, however, does close the play
frame, reaffirming the essentially paradoxical nature
of the episode by pointing out, in its content, that the
"Did you hear it?" question was not in earnest after
all.   Furthermore, by its content, it reopens the whole
subject of sounds and smells that had been so effectively hidden in the roses.   And we find out that "Did you
hear it?" was really part of the punch line, drawn out
in this skillful manner.

One further phenomenon needs comment before concluding this excursion through the world of humor.

That phenomenon is the terminal laugh. If a laugh
starts in the body of the joke and becomes too much
primary and too little secondary, or too much mood and
too little message, the humor is vitiated for the audience. The terminal laugh is a different matter. A
boisterous, genuine laugh is the desired prize of all
jokers. A cue laugh or metaphoric laugh—although
humor-potentiating when offered during the process of
presentation—is entirely out of place at the end of a
joke and can completely puncture the bag of humor if
it is contrived as a punch-line reaction (unless it may
be itself a punch line).

The metaphoric terminal laugh carries with it a
message which could be summarized as "You have told
me a story which was presented as a joke, and, although
I am trying to laugh for your sake, the joke is such
that I can't laugh, even though I want to for you." This
laugh is an instrument rather than a mood. It brings
too uncomfortably close the aspect of life from which
humor is so admirably suited as an escape. The metaphoric laugh has a lineal relationship with laughter, but
is actually antihumorous.

The more metacommunicative or metaphoric the
terminal laugh becomes, the weaker would seem to be
the quality of the humor involved. It is true that all
laughs have a metacommunicative nature which is essential to their significance as human behavior. This
cannot be denied. But generally, the preponderance of
"primariness" or "mood" over metaphor or signaling
in a terminal laugh is desirable in both audience and
joker. It is quite painful when a joke has failed of its
humor goal and the audience nevertheless tries to emit
mood laughter, which comes out as humor-signaling
laughter and is a lie because there is little humor to
signal about. The laughter then is a two-times fraud,
and audience and joker both silently cross that joke off
their lists.

And so, the final paradox is that when the terminal
laugh is consciously used to communicate humor, it
fails of its purpose and conveys quite a different

impression, and when it arises spontaneously from an impulse of humor and the communication of amusement is not intended, it succeeds in the communication of humor quite fully—sometimes even to the extent that persons around, although unaware of the cause of laughter, will become infected with the gaiety also.

How many times does a person—with good intentions and a stout heart—set out to make the world around him a happier place in which to live? Only to find that he has tried too hard. His laugh—formed with open mouth and shaking head—came too much as a copy of Nature and too little as Nature itself. How many of his paintings, his songs, and stories, how many of his tears and sobs—how much of his life is so contrived and fabricated with the life-threads that it becomes fraud or copy and he struts through a dream that is no longer a dream but has now come alive! For it is important—and to express it tortures the whole structure of what I am trying to convey here—that Life is Life—primary process, metaphor, and all. In the larger sense, metaphor is statement of a mood, as is the spontaneous laugh, in that it is, as is that which we seem to perceive in the skies and name as stars all part of the larger, infinity-sized ongoing life.

All of which makes, among other things, writing such books as this so difficult. When you put a butterfly on a pin, he soon is dead.

Finally, in these thoughts, I reaffirm my belief in the central mystery of the nature of those human phenomena of which humor is an example. I feel that paradox is as close to the central mystery as it has been possible to move. Whenever man seeks to inspect the self, he will confront the self and discover that the self is the inspector. Perhaps this paradox is responsible for some of the great excitement and satisfaction that can come to us from studies of our human nature.

Bibliography

Aird, R. B., Gordon, N. S., and Gregg, H. C., Use of
Phenacemide (Phenurone) in Treatment of Narcolepsy
and Cataplexy, A.M.A. Archives of Neurology and
Psychiatry, 70:510, 1953.

Albino, R. C., Defenses Against Aggression in the Play
of Young Children, British Journal of Medical Psychology, 27:61, 1954.

Allee, W. C., Cooperation Among Animals. New York:
Henry Schuman, rev. ed., 1951.

Bachrack, A. J., Notes on the Psychopathology of Delu-
sions, Psychiatry, 16:4, 1953.

Bateson, Gregory, Further Notes on a Snake Dance of
the Baining, Oceania II, 3:334, 1932.

_____, Social Planning and the Concept of "Deutero-
Learning," in Conference on Science, Philosophy, and
Religion, Second Symposium, 81-97. New York:
Harper, 1942.

_____, The Pattern of an Armaments Race, Bulletin
of the Atomic Scientists, 2:10, 1946.

_____, The Position of Humor in Human Communica-
tion, in Cybernetics, Ninth Conference, ed. Heinz von
Foerster. The Josiah Macy, Jr. Foundation, 1952.

_____, Why Do Frenchmen, Etc., 10:127, 1953.

_____, About Games and Being Serious, Etc., 10:213,
1953.

_____, Why Do Things Have Outlines? Etc., 11:59,
1953.

_____, A Theory of Play and Fantasy, Psychiatric
Research Reports, American Psychiatric Association, 2:39, 1955.

_____, The Message "This Is Play," in Group Proc-
esses, Second Conference, ed. Bertram Schaffner.
Josiah Macy, Jr., Foundation, 1956.

Bateson, Gregory and Ruesch, Jurgen. Communication:
The Social Matrix of Psychiatry. New York: W. W.
Norton & Co., Inc., 1951.

Bateson, Gregory, Jackson, D. D., Haley, J., Weakland, J., Toward a Theory of Schizophrenia, Behavioral Science, 1:251, 1956.

Bateson, Gregory, and Kees, W., The Nature of Play (a film).

Bergler, E., Laughter and the Sense of Humor. New York: Intercontinental Medical Book Corp., 1956.

Brenman, Margaret, On Teasing and Being Teased, in The Psychoanalytic Study of the Child, VII, 1952. New York: International Universities Press.

Cave, H. A., Narcolepsy, Archives of Neurology and Psychiatry, 26:50, 1931.

Cohn, R., Forced Crying and Laughing, Archives of Neurology and Psychiatry, 66:738, 1951.

Collingwood, R. G., Principles of Art, London: Oxford University Press, 1938.

Craik, K. J. W., The Nature of Explanation, Cambridge: Cambridge University Press, 1943.

Darwin, Charles, Expression of the Emotions in Man and Animals, London: John Murray, Ltd., 1872.

Davison, C., and Kelman, H., Pathologic Laughing and Crying, Archives of Neurology and Psychiatry, 42: 595, 1939.

Drake, F. R., Narcolepsy: Brief Review and Report of Cases, American Journal of Medical Sciences, 218: 101, 1949.

Dynes, John B., Narcolepsy and Cataplexy, Lahey Clinic Bulletin, 2:83, 1941.

_____, Cataplexy and Its Treatment, Journal of Nervous and Mental Diseases, 98:48, 1943.

Eastman, Max, Enjoyment of Laughter, London: Hamish Hamilton, 1937.

Ehrenzweig, A., The Psychoanalysis of Artistic Vision and Hearing, New York: Julian Press, 1953.

Fabing, H. D., Narcolepsy, Archives of Neurology and Psychiatry, 54:367, 1945.

_____, Narcolepsy, Archives of Neurology and Psychiatry, 55:353, 1946.

Fowler, H. W., Modern English Usage, Oxford: Clarendon Press, 1926.

Freud, Sigmund, Wit and Its Relation to the Unconscious, tr. A. A. Brill. London: Kegan Paul, 1916.

Friedman, L. J., Defensive Aspects of Orality, International Journal of Psychoanalysis, 34:304, 1953.

Gerard, R. W., Some of the Problems Concerning Digital Notions in the Central Nervous System, in Cybernetics, Seventh Conference. The Josiah Macy, Jr. Foundation, 1950.

Gordon, B. L., Medicine Throughout Antiquity. Philadelphia: F. A. Davis Co., 1949.

Gorer, Geoffrey, The American People. New York: W. W. Norton & Co., Inc., 1948.

Graves, Robert, Mrs. Fisher, or The Future of Humour. London: Kegan Paul, Trench, Trubner & Co., Ltd., 1928.

Greenacre, Phillis, Swift and Carroll: A Psychoanalytic Study of Two Lives. New York: International Universities Press, 1955.

Greig, J. Y. T., The Psychology of Laughter and Comedy. New York: Dodd, Mead & Co., 1923.

Grotjahn, M., Laughter in Dreams, Psychoanalytic Quarterly, 13:221, 1945.

_____, Beyond Laughter. New York: McGraw-Hill, 1957.

Haley, J., Communication and the Film. (unpublished).

_____, Paradoxes in Play, Fantasy and Psychotherapy, Psychiatric Research Reports, American Psychiatric Association, 2:52, 1955.

Harms, E., The Development of Humor. Journal of Abnormal and Social Psychology, 38:351, 1943.

Harrison, J. E., Themis: A Study of the Social Origins of Greek Religion. Cambridge: Cambridge University Press, 1927.

Hastorf, A. H. and Cantril, H., They Saw a Game, Journal of Abnormal and Social Psychology, 49:129, 1954.

Herrigel, Eugene, Zen in the Art of Archery. New York: Pantheon Books, 1953.

Huxley, Aldous, The Doors of Perception. New York: Harper & Bros., 1954.

Jackson, D. D., An Episode of Sleepwalking, Journal American Psychoanalytic Association, 2:503, 1954.

Jacobson, E., The Child's Laughter, in The Psychoanalytic Study of the Child. II. New York: International University Press, 1946.

Justin, F., A Genetic Study of Laughter-Provoking Stimuli, Child Development, 3-4:114, 1932-33.

Kant, O., Inappropriate Laughter and Silliness in Schizophrenia, Journal of Abnormal and Social Psychology, 37:398, 1942.

Kasanin, J. S., ed., Language and Thought in Schizophrenia. Berkeley: University of California Press, 1946.

Kofoid, C. A., ed., Termites and Termite Control. Berkeley: University of California Press, 1934.

Kris, Ernst, Psychoanalytic Explorations in Art. New York: International Universities Press, 1952.

Levin, M., Aggression, Guilt and Cataplexy, Archives of Neurology and Psychiatry, 69:224, 1953.

Locke, W., and Bailey, A. A., Narcolepsy, Report of an Unusual Case, Proceedings of the Mayo Clinic, 15:491, 1940.

Lorenz, Konrad Z., King Solomon's Ring. New York: Thomas Y. Crowell Co., 1952.

Lowes, John L., The Road to Xanadu. Boston: Houghton Mifflin Co., 1927.

Ludovici, Anthony M., The Secret of Laughter. London: Constable & Co., Ltd., 1932.

Malinowski, Bronislaw, Argonauts of the Western Pacific. London: George Routledge & Sons, Ltd., 1922.

Marmor, Judd, Orality in the Hysterical Personality, Journal of American Psychoanalytic Association, 1:656, 1953.

Martin, J. P., Fits of Laughter in Organic Cerebral Disease, Brain, 73:453, 1950.

McCabe, Thomas T., and Blanchard, Barbara D., Three Species of Peromyscus. Rood Association, 1950.

McDougall, William, A New Theory of Laughter, Psyche, 2 (n.s.), 1922.

Munro, D. H., Argument of Laughter. Melbourne: Melbourne University Press, 1951.

Nagel, E., and Newman, J. R., Godel's Proof, Scientific American, 194:71, 1956.

Nicoll, Allardyce, Masks, Mimes and Miracles. London: George G. Harrap & Co., Ltd., 1931.

Oates, W. J., and O'Neill, Eugene, Jr., eds., The Complete Greek Drama. New York: Random House, 1938.

Reich, A., Structure of the Grotesque-Comic Sublimation, Bulletin of the Menninger Clinic, 131:160, 1949.

Rosenblueth, A., Wiener, N., and Bigelow, J., Behavior, Purpose, and Teleology, Journal of Philosophical Sciences, 10:18, 1943.

Roubicek, Jiri, Laughter in Epilepsy, Journal of Mental Sciences, 92:734, 1946.

Schwartz, E. K., A Psychoanalytic Study of the Fairy Tale, American Journal of Psychotherapy, 10(4):740, 1956.

Seward, Samuel S., Jr., The Paradox of the Ludicrous. Stanford: Stanford University Press, 1930.

Sewell, Elizabeth, The Field of Nonsense. London: Chatto & Windus, 1952.

Smith, H. Allen, Compleat Practical Joker. New York: Doubleday, 1953.

Sperling, S. J., On the Psychodynamics of Teasing, Journal of American Psychoanalytic Association, 3:458, 1953.

Spiegelman, M., Terwilliger, C., and Fearing, F., The Content of Comics, Journal of Social Psychology, 37:189, 1953.

Sullivan, H. S., Clinical Studies in Psychiatry, New York: W. W. Norton & Co., Inc., 1956.

Suzuki, D. T., Studies in Zen. New York: Philosophical Library, 1955.

Thomson, J. Oliver, History of Ancient Geography. Cambridge: Cambridge University Press, 1948.

Tinbergen, N., The Study of Instinct. Oxford: Clarendon Press, 1951.

_____, Social Behavior in Animals. Methuen, 1953.

Washburn, R. W., A Study of the Smiling and Laughing
    of Infants in the First Year of Life, Genetic Psy-
    chology Monographs, 6:397, 1929.
Weakland, J. H., Orality in Chinese Concepts of Male
    Genital Sexuality, Psychiatry, 19(3):237, 1956.
Whitehead, Alfred North, and Russell, Bertrand. Prin-
    cipia Mathematica. Cambridge: Cambridge University
    Press, 1910.
Whitehead, Alfred North, The Philosophy of Alfred North
    Whitehead, ed. P. A. Schilpp. Chicago: Northwestern
    University Press, 1941.
_____, Essays in Science and Philosophy. New York:
    Philosophical Library, 1947.
Wiener, Norbert, The Human Use of Human Beings.
    Boston: Houghton Mifflin Co., 1950.
Wilcox, D. E., Observations of Speech Disturbances in
    Childhood Schizophrenia, Diseases of the Nervous
    System, 17(1):20, 1956.
Wilson, S. A. Kinnier. Neurology. Ed. A. Ninian
    Bruce. Baltimore: Williams & Wilkins Co., 1940.
Wittgenstein, Ludwig, Philosophical Investigations. Tr.
    G. E. M. Anscombe. New York: Macmillan, 1953.
Wolfenstein, Martha, and Leites, Nathan. Movies. Chi-
    cago: Free Press, 1950.
Wolfenstein, Martha, Children's Humor. Chicago: Free
    Press, 1954.
Young, P. T., Emotions in Man and Animal. New York:
    Wiley, 1943.